Abingdon's

Bible ZONE LIVE

Where the Bible Comes to Life

On the Road

Older Elementary

Also available from Abingdon Press:

Abingdon's BibleZone® LIVE
Preschool
FUNspirational® Kit

Abingdon's BibleZone® LIVE
Younger Elementary
FUNspirational® Kit

Writer: Delia Halverson
Editor: James H. Ritchie, Jr.
Production Editor: Betsi Smith
Production and Design Manager:
R.E. Osborne
Designer: Paige Easter
Front Cover Photo: Ron Benedict
Back Cover Photo: Ron Benedict
Illustrator: Susan Harrison
Illustrator: Doug Jones

Abingdon's

Bible ZONE LIVE

Older Elementary

where the Bible Comes to Life

ON THE ROAD

Abingdon Press
Nashville

Abingdon's
BibleZone® LIVE
Where the Bible Comes to Life
ON THE ROAD
Older Elementary

Unless otherwise noted, Scripture quotations are from the Contemporary English Version, © 1991, 1992, 1995 by the American Bible Society. Used by permission.

Scripture quotations identified as Good News Translation are from the Good News Translation in Today's English Version—Second Edition. Copyright © 1992 American Bible Society. Used by permission.

ISBN 0-687-09450-X

Compact Disc Credits:
"The Servant Song," © 1977 Scripture in Song (a div. of Integrity Music, Inc.). "Hosanna to the King!" © 2001 Abingdon Press, admin. by the Copyright Co., Nashville, TN. "Shout 'Hosanna!'" words © 1999 Abingdon Press, admin. by The Copyright Co., Nashville, TN 37212. "Donkey Music," © 2000 Cokesbury. "Jesu, Jesu," © 1969 and 1989 Hope Publishing Co. "Were You There?" adapt. and arr. © 1989 The United Methodist Publishing House. "Love One Another," music © 1991 Graded Press, admin. by The Copyright Co., Nashville, TN. "Hallelujah Chorus," © 2002 Abingdon Press, admin. by The Copyright Co., Nashville, TN 37212. "Where Is Jesus?" words © 2002 Cokesbury, admin. by The Copyright Co., Nashville, TN 37212. "We Remember You," © 2002 Abingdon Press, admin. by The Copyright Co., Nashville, TN 37212. "The Summons," words © 1987 WGRG The Iona Community (Scotland), admin. by GIA Publications Inc. "Two by Two," words © 1996 Cokesbury. "It Is Good to Give Thanks," © 2003 Abingdon Press, admin. by The Copyright Co., Nashville, TN 37212. "Thank You, God," © 2001 Cokesbury. "Affirming Music" © 2001 Cokesbury. "Zacchaeus, Come Down From That Tree," © 2001 Cokesbury. "Zacchaeus Was a Wee Little Man," arr. © 1993 Abingdon Press. "One of a Kind," © 2004 Abingdon Press. "Go, Bartimaeus," Words and music © 1991 by James Ritchie. Arrangement © 1995 Cokesbury. "Sing! Shout! Turn About!" sts. 2–3 and music © 1993 Cokesbury; st. 1 © 1999 Cokesbury. "It Makes No Difference," words © 1994, CRC Publications; music © 1994 Sean E. Ivory. "I Can Tell," words © 2000 Cokesbury, admin. by The Copyright Co., Nashville, TN. "I Am a 'C,'" arr. © 1980 Lillenas Publishing Company (SESAC). All rights reserved. Administered by The Copyright Company, 40 Music Square East, Nashville, TN 37203. "A Christian I Will Be," music arr. © 1988 Graded Press. "Attention! Attention!" © 2006 Abingdon Press. "I Am on the Road With Jesus," © 2005 Abingdon Press. "Let's Praise the Lord," © 2005 Abingdon Press. "The Stinky Feet Song," © 2000 Roger Day. Narration: "Thank You in Several Languages," recording © 2005 Abingdon Press.

Art on pages 40, 44, 68, 92, 104, 160, 164, 166, 167 by Doug Jones; art on pages 20, 26, 32, 50, 52, 56, 64, 80, 87, 88, 99, 100, 111, 112, 116, 124, 136, 140, 148, 152 and Transparencies 1–3 by Susan Harrison. © 2005 Abingdon Press.

05 06 07 08 09 10 11 12 13 14—10 9 8 7 6 5 4 3 2 1
MANUFACTURED IN THE UNITED STATES OF AMERICA

Table of Contents

On the Road

Bible Units in the Zone 6

About BibleZone® Live 7

Welcome to BibleZone® Live 8

Older Elementary 9

First and Last 10

Palm Sunday 22

Jesus Serves 34

The Saddest Day 46

Out of the Tomb 58

The Emmaus Road 70

Two by Two 82

Ten Lepers 94

Zacchaeus 106

Blind Bartimaeus 118

The Damascus Road 130

Philip and the Ethiopian 142

Barnabas 154

Puppet Accessories (Lesson 3) 166

Number Cube (Lesson 13) 168

Game Cards (Lesson 13) 169

Nametags 170

GameZone 171

ArtZone 172

May I Join You? (Lesson 6) 173

Closing Prayers 174

Comments From Users 175

Bible Units in the  _____

On the Road to Easter

Bible Story	Bible Verse
First and Last	Mark 10:43
Palm Sunday	Mark 11:9
Jesus Serves	John 13:15
The Saddest Day	Romans 8:32
Out of the Tomb	Psalm 99:3
The Emmaus Road	Acts 2:32

On the Road With Jesus

Bible Story	Bible Verse
Two by Two	1 Corinthians 3:9a, Good News Translation
Ten Lepers	Luke 17:19
Zacchaeus	Luke 19:10
Blind Bartimaeus	Matthew 7:11

Followers of Jesus on the Road

Bible Story	Bible Verse
The Damascus Road	Romans 15:16, adapted
Philip and the Ethiopian	Psalm 25:4
Barnabas	1 Thessalonians 5:14

About Bible ZONE LIVE

ZoneZillies:

ZoneZillies® are game and storytelling props found in the BibleZone® FUNspirational® Kit. Some ZoneZillies® are consumable and will need to be replaced. These are added for the teacher's convenience.

- CD
- tape measure key chains
- bouncing rock balls
- click pen necklaces
- striped beach balls
- inflatable palm tree
- spiked rubber ball with pump
- train whistle

Supplies:

- Bible for each student (include one *Contemporary English Version*)
- CD player
- small table
- white tablecloth
- colored fabric
- candle
- scissors
- paper, construction paper, newspaper, self-adhesive notes, paper with a glossy surface
- crayons, markers, transparency marker, pencils, chalk
- tempera paint, watercolor paint, paintbrushes
- tape, masking tape, safety pins, glue
- iron
- baking sheet
- basin and towel
- basket
- beeswax sheets, candle wicks
- blindfolds
- bookmarks
- brown lunch-size paper bags
- chalkboard, markerboard, or large pieces of paper
- cleanup supplies
- closed box with mirror on the inside
- dishwashing soap
- dry bulb or onion, unsliced loaf of bread
- envelopes
- eye droppers or spoons
- flat plain cookies
- game pieces
- index cards
- magazines
- mirror
- poster or article with *JOY* on it
- posterboard
- plastic wrap
- plastic spoons
- plastic drinking straws
- old cookie sheets, skillet
- overhead projector
- piece of wood showing growth circles
- rocks
- rags
- ruler
- running shoes, sandals
- sandpaper
- small bowls
- small plastic flowers
- thank-you card
- tube icing, decorating tips
- water
- wax paper
- tray or shallow dishes
- plastic cups
- optional: biblical costumes, plain shower curtain or bed sheet, erasable markers, polyurethane spray, rhythm instruments, permanent markers

Welcome to BibleZONE LIVE

Where the Bible Comes to Life

Have fun learning about favorite Bible stories from the Old and New Testaments. Each lesson in this teacher guide is filled with games and activities that will make learning FUNspirational® for you and your students. With just a few added supplies, everything you need to teach is included in the Abingdon's BibleZone® Live FUNspirational® Kit.

Each lesson has a ZoneIn® box:

 God wants us to share our gifts and talents with others.

that is repeated over and over again throughout the lesson. The ZoneIn® states the Bible message in words your students will connect to their lives.

Use the following tips to help make your trip into BibleZone® Live a FUNspirational® success!

- Read through each lesson. Read the Bible passages.
- Memorize the Bible verse and the ZoneIn® statement.
- Choose the activities that fit your unique group of students and your time limitations.
- Read the BibleZone® story.
- Gather the ZoneZillies® you will use for the lesson.
- Gather supplies you will use for the lesson.
- Learn the music for the lesson from the BibleZone® FUNspirational® CD.
- Arrange your room space so there is plenty of room for the students to move and sit on the floor.
- Photocopy the Reproducible pages for the lesson.
- Photocopy the HomeZone® page for students.
- Photocopy any illustrations (pages 166–174).

8

Older Elementary

Each child in your class is a one-of-a-kind child of God. Each child has his or her own name, background, family situation, and set of experiences. It is important to remember and celebrate the uniqueness of each child. Yet all of these one-of-a-kind children of God have some common needs.

- All children need love.
- All children need a sense of self-worth.
- All children need to feel a sense of accomplishment.
- All children need to have a safe place to be and to express their feelings.
- All children need to be surrounded by adults who love them.
- All children need to experience the love of God.

Older Elementary students (ages 9–12 years old) also have some common characteristics.

Their Bodies
- They are experiencing rapid physical and emotional changes.
- Their growing takes a lot of energy, sometimes leaving them lethargic.
- There are great variations of emotional and physical growth among older elementary age students. They are different from one another and different from who they were just a short time ago.

Their Minds
- They are concrete thinkers.
- They are practical planners, working toward logical conclusions.
- They like to identify and express attitudes, ideas, and feelings about unfairness and unjust treatment of people.
- They like to laugh and can be silly.
- They are ready for challenging Bible skills and activities.
- They are ready to increase and use vocabulary related to the Christian faith.
- They are capable of understanding people and places unknown to them.

Their Relationships
- They desire to be similar to all their friends but recognize they are not.
- They may have trouble accepting themselves and others at different stages of their personal development.
- They adopt adult language and can appear to be sophisticated.
- They do not want to appear to be vulnerable or innocent.
- They are beginning to identify themselves as individuals separate from their families.

Their Hearts
- They need caring adults who model Christian attitudes and behaviors.
- They need to verbalize experiences and questions about God and faith.
- They need to serve with others in the community and the world.
- They need to feel they have a personal relationship with God.
- They need a sense of belonging to the church and to the larger faith community.

First and Last

Enter the

Bible Verse

If you want to be great, you must be the servant of all the others.

Mark 10:43

Bible Story
Mark 10:35-45

Matthew's version of this story (20:20-28), most likely based on Mark's account written earlier, has the mother of James and John requesting honored seats in Jesus' kingdom for her sons, rather than having them ask directly, as they do in Mark's Gospel. Was Matthew attempting to soften the disciples' blind ambition with motherly pride? If so, it doesn't work. The brothers' quick response to the "Are you able?" question indicates that the original right-hand/left-hand question was their own, not their mother's.

The angry response of the other ten proves that they saw the kingdom as governmental rule, with them as chief ministers of state, not as humble servants of the good news. Jesus brought them up short, asserting that in order to be a leader in this kingdom, one must be a slave. Right ambition is a desire to follow Christ's leading, and prominence in the kingdom comes from a willingness to give Christ and others priority.

Then there are the baptism and cup metaphors. At a royal banquet the king customarily handed a cup to special guests. Jesus used this act to warn his disciples that being in his service required a willingness to take some of the same treatment—both the blessing and curse—that he himself would receive. His reference to baptism—literally, to be submerged in an experience—is an invitation for his disciples to immerse themselves in the hatred and pain that Jesus would soon fall victim to. He was alerting them to the ridicule, rejection, and physical danger that would be their "reward" if they dedicated themselves to following him.

Power and prestige are not new inventions, though our society seems to be universally enamored with the powerful and the prestigious. Children grow up wanting to control their lives rather than to sacrifice control to persons with broader knowledge and experience. We are challenged to help them identify those persons and that God to whom they can safely relinquish control.

Followers of Jesus put others first.

Scope the

ZONE	TIME	SUPPLIES	⊚ ZONEZILLIES®
Zoom Into the Zone			
Get in the Zone	5 minutes	page 170, tape or safety pins, CD player	CD
Celebration Table	10 minutes	page 174, scissors, colored fabric, small table, candle, white tablecloth, Bible, poster or article with *JOY* on it	none
BibleZone®			
On the Road	5 minutes	Bibles	spiked rubber ball
Enjoy the Story	10 minutes	Reproducibles 1A–1B	none
Bouncing Bible Verse	5 minutes	chalkboard, markerboard or large piece of paper; chalk or markers	striped beach ball, train whistle, spiked rubber ball
J.O.Y. Posters	5 minutes	Reproducible 1C, markers	spiked rubber ball
LifeZone			
First and Last Poem	5 minutes	Reproducible 1D	click pen necklaces, spiked rubber ball
Learn a Song	5 minutes	Reproducible 1E, CD player	CD, tape measure key chains
Praise 'n Prayer	10 minutes	Celebration Table, poster or article with *JOY* printed on it, page 174	none

⊚ ZoneZillies® are found in the **BibleZone® LIVE FUNspirational® Kit.**

Zoom Into the Zone

Choose one or more activities to catch your children's interest.

Supplies:
page 170
tape or safety pins
CD player

ZoneZillies®:
CD

Supplies:
page 174
scissors
small table
white tablecloth
colored fabric
candle
Bible
poster or article with
   "JOY" printed on it

ZoneZillies®:
none

Get in the Zone

Play "Jesu, Jesu" **(CD)** as the students arrive. Greet each student with a happy smile. If the students do not know one another, give them all nametags to wear (page 170).

Say: Welcome to BibleZone Live! I'm glad you are here. This is the fun place where we will get to know the Bible as our book!

Celebration Table

Ask one of the students who arrives early to help you prepare the Celebration Table. Cover a small table or card table with a white tablecloth. In the center place a piece of fabric that corresponds to the Christian season:

Season	Time	Color	Meaning
Advent	4 Sundays before Christmas	purple/blue	royalty of Christ/hope
Christmas	Christmas Eve until Epiphany	white/gold	purity/royalty
Epiphany/ Ordinary	Jan. 6 to Lent	green	growth
Lent	Ash Wednesday to Easter	purple	penitence
Easter	Easter to Pentecost	white	purity
Pentecost	50 days after Easter	red	fire of Holy Spirit

(Some churches continue using Pentecost colors several weeks.)

Season	Time	Color	Meaning
Ordinary Time	between Pentecost and Advent	green	growth

(The term "ordinary" means in order.)

Add a candle and a Bible. For this session place a poster or some article with *JOY* printed on it beside the candle.

Photocopy and cut apart the closing prayer slips (page 174). Each week ask a student to prepare to read one during your Praise 'n Prayer time. Give a student the prayer for week one.

12

Choose one or more activities to immerse your children in the Bible story.

On the Road

Supplies:
Bibles

ZoneZillies®:
spiked rubber ball

Sit together in a circle as you introduce the "On the Road" unit.

Say: Welcome! Our theme this quarter is "On the Road." Our stories will have some connection with a road or with people traveling—physically traveling or simply moving in the direction of becoming a better Christian. During this quarter we will be working with the part of the Bible called the New Testament, written after the time of Jesus' ministry on earth.

Ask the students to find the beginning of the New Testament. Tell them that one way to find the New Testament is to find the center of the Bible and then the center of the back half of the Bible. This should put them close to the beginning of the New Testament. Remind them that Matthew is the first book in the New Testament.

Say: In the first ten sessions we will learn about stories from the first four books of the New Testament—the ones we call Gospels or "Good News." (*Ask them to find Matthew, Mark, Luke, and John, and then to turn to the end of John.*) **After the Gospel of John comes the Book of Acts, the story of how the first Christians formed churches after Jesus died and was resurrected. The last three sessions of this quarter will come from the Book of Acts.**

Hold up the **spiked rubber ball.**

Say: This is something that we will use to help us with our discussion this quarter. We will use it when we have conversations like this one. Each time you want to talk, raise your hand and the spiked ball will be tossed to you. Only the person holding the spiked ball will talk. That way we can all listen to what is being said. Let's try this out. Everyone will have a chance now to first give your name and then tell about some road trip you've been on. It doesn't have to be a trip far away. When you are ready to share, raise your hand and I will toss the spiked ball to you. Say your name and tell about a road trip; then toss the ball to someone else whose hand is raised.

Enjoy the Story

Supplies:
Reproducibles 1A–1B

ZoneZillies®:
none

Hand out **Reproducibles 1A–1B** and ask volunteers to read the parts of James and John.

First and Last

(based on Mark 10:35-45)

by Delia Halverson

James: My name is James.

John: And my name is John. James and I are brothers.

James & John: We're sons of the fisherman, Zebedee.

James: We want to tell you about something special that we learned from a man called Jesus.

John: Some time back when we were mending our fishing nets on the Sea of Galilee, Jesus stopped to talk. Jesus asked us to leave our nets and come with him to help him teach others about God's love. After traveling with him for about three years, we truly believe that he is the long-awaited Messiah.

James: We always believed that God would send a Messiah to save our people. But it seems that the Messiah we had in mind was not the Messiah God had in mind.

John: We were expecting our Messiah to break the power that Rome has over us and replace Roman rule with his own kingdom.

James: One day we came up to Jesus and asked him a favor—a big favor.

John: "Teacher," we asked, "when you come into your glory, please let one of us sit at your right side and the other at your left."

James: The expression on Jesus' face matched his words. "You don't really know what you are asking! Are you able to drink from the cup that I must soon drink from? Are you able to be baptized as I must be baptized?"

John: Hmmm, we thought. Good question! We'd already been through a lot with him, and we figured that we ought to be able to follow his example. So we both answered him . . .

James & John: Yes, we are!

James: Jesus assured us that we would surely do that, but then he said, "But it isn't for me to say who will sit at my right side and at my left. That is for God to decide."

John: I'm afraid we made the other disciples angry with our request.

James: Jesus said that we shouldn't act like the kings who order their people around with great power over their people. I guess that's the sort of kingdom that we had in mind.

14

Reproducible 1A

John: Were we ever wrong! That's not the sort of kingdom that Jesus will rule. We learned that with the next thing that Jesus said.

James: Jesus said something that we will remember the rest of our lives.

John: "If you want to be great, you must be the servant of all the others."

James: "If you want to be first, you must be everyone's slave."

John: Then Jesus added, "The Son of Man (that's what Jesus called himself) did not come to be a slave master, but a slave who will give his life to rescue many people."

James: There isn't much glory in being a slave, and glory was what we were looking for!

John: Do you think you could be a servant—or even a slave to others?

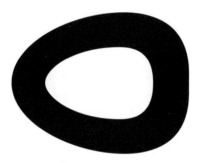

If you want to be great, you must be the servant of all the others. (Mark 10:43)

Reproducible 1C

BIBLEZONE® LIVE

Choose one or more activities to immerse your children in the Bible story.

Bouncing Bible Verse

Write the Bible verse on the chalkboard, dry erase board, or a large piece of paper in three segments:

If you want to be great/you must be the servant/of all the others. (Mark 10:43)

Have the students stand in a circle. Hand one student the **striped beach ball**. Have the **train whistle** on hand.

Say: We are going to learn our Bible verse by passing the ball around the circle. The first person will gently toss the ball to the person on his or her left and say, "If you want to be great." The second person will gently toss the ball to the next person and say, "you must be the servant." The next person will catch the ball and toss it to the next person saying, "of all the others. (Mark 10:43)." The next person then starts over. Continue until I blow the train whistle.

Give the students the opportunity to say their verse several times before you blow the whistle. Then, erase the verse and have everyone repeat it together three times. After you have practiced the verse, ask the questions listed below, using the **spiked rubber ball** to initiate discussion.

Ask: In your school classroom, what job do you see as the most important? What jobs are the least important? What does our Bible verse say about this?

Supplies:
chalkboard, dry erase board, or large paper
chalk or markers

ZoneZillies®:
striped beach balls
train whistle
spiked rubber ball

J.O.Y. Posters

Hand out **Reproducible 1C** and markers. Tell the students that they are to create a poster that they can put in their rooms at home to remind them of the Bible verse. Invite each student to illustrate or write some action that they can do for Jesus under the *J*, some action they can do for others under the *O*, and some action they can do for themselves under the *Y*.

After the posters are complete, use the **spiked rubber ball** to initiate discussion about what the students illustrated or wrote. Make note that the three letters spell out *JOY* and tell them that according to our story today the way to have joy is to put Jesus first, others second, and yourself last.

Supplies:
Reproducible 1C
markers

ZoneZillies®:
spiked rubber ball

Choose one or more activities to bring the Bible to life.

Supplies:
Reproducible 1D

ZoneZillies®:
click pen necklaces
spiked rubber ball

First and Last Poem

Hand out **Reproducible 1D** and the **click pen necklaces**. Be sure that the students understand the directions.

After the acrostic poems are complete, invite the students to share their sentences using the **spiked rubber ball** to take turns.

Supplies:
Reproducible 1E
CD player

ZoneZillies®:
CD
tape measure key chains

Learn a Song

Hand out **Reproducible 1E**, "The Servant Song," and the **tape measure key chains**. Invite the students to listen as you play the song **(CD, Track 1)** and to "measure" the height of the notes.

Say: Hold the tape measure case in one hand with your finger on the release button while grasping the end of the tape in the other hand. Test how far you can extend the tape between the case, held low, and the end of the tape measure, held high. This distance represents the highest note in the song—the second note on the third line (*that*). **Next, retract the tape completely. This represents the lowest note—the next-to-last note in the verse (the second syllable of** *servant***).**

Play the song and have the students "measure" each note as they listen. Tell the students that you will use this song as a gathering signal throughout the quarter. When the song begins, everyone is to begin singing it and moving to the Celebration Table for Praise 'n Prayer time. Have the students set the measuring tapes aside and then play the song again to let the children practice gathering for Praise 'n Prayer time.

Supplies:
Celebration Table
poster or article with
  JOY printed on it
page 174

ZoneZillies®:
none

Praise 'n Prayer

Light the candle and call the students' attention to the appropriate seasonal color and the poster or article with *JOY* on it that is on the table. Ask them to recall what the letters *J-O-Y* stand for.

Ask the student you assigned earlier to close with the following prayer (also on page 174): "O God, make us willing to serve rather than asking to be served, and help us find the joy of putting Jesus first, others second, and ourselves last. Amen."

Make a copy of HomeZone® for each student in your class.

18

THANK YOU, GOD

Make a chart to help you recognize the times that you've acted in ways that Jesus taught us to act. Divide a paper into two columns. At the top of one column write, "Thank you, God, for the chance to serve you and others by acting this way." At the top of the other column, write, "I'm sorry, God, for insisting that others serve me by acting this way."

During the week fill in the form, but do not show it to others. Keep it where you can find it each night and either thank God or ask for God's forgiveness.

ThinkZone

How different would the world be if everyone put Jesus first, others second, and themselves last?

Memory Verse

If you want to be great, you must be the servant of all the others.

Mark 10:43

Joy Cookies

Make a basic sugar cookie dough and roll it out. Cut only a dozen cookies at a time so that the unbaked cookies won't dry out before they are painted. Place the cookies on a cookie sheet. Prepare Egg Yolk Paint from the recipe below. Using small paintbrushes, paint the letters *JOY* on the cookies. Be sure to put the periods after the letters to remind you that the letters stand for *Jesus first, Others second*, and *Yourself last*. Bake as directed in the recipe. Be sure that the cookies don't brown in order to keep the colors clear.

Egg Yolk Paint: Blend 1 egg yolk with ½ teaspoon water. You may divide the mixture into three bowls or cups if you want more than one color. Add enough food coloring to each cup to make the color bright. If the paint thickens add a few drops of water.

Alternative: Buy prepared cookies and tubes of colored icing.

Followers of Jesus put others first.

Followers of Jesus

Jesus told us how we should act. On the blanks below, write a sentence about how you can act kindly toward someone else. Use the letters printed at the beginning of each line as the first letter in the sentence.

F _____

I _____

R _____

S _____

T _____

shall be

L _____

A _____

S _____

T _____

and the last shall be first.

SECOND HARVEST FOOD BANK

Reproducible 1D

BibleZone® LIVE

The Servant Song

Brother, sister, let me serve you,
let me be as Christ to you;
pray that I may have the grace
to let you be my servant, too.

We are pilgrims on a journey;
we're together on this road.
We are here to help each other
walk the mile and bear the load.

WORDS: Richard Gillard (Matt. 20:26)
MUSIC: Richard Gillard
© 1977 Scripture in Song (a div. of Integrity Music, Inc.)

OLDER ELEMENTARY: LESSON 1   **Reproducible 1E**
Permission granted to photocopy for local church use. © 2005 Abingdon Press.

Palm Sunday

Enter the **ZONE**

Bible Verse

God bless the one who comes in the name of the Lord!

Mark 11:9

Bible Story

Mark 11:1-11

What does Jesus' triumphal entry into Jerusalem mean? If Mark is correct and this was the first time during the course of Jesus' ministry that Jesus visited Jerusalem, then how did he arrange for the donkey? But, if John is correct, then Jesus had already visited the city on several occasions. Remember that the Gospel writers were not writing a timeline of Jesus' life, but a message of good news intended to inspire their readers. Matthew, Mark, and Luke seem to cluster stories of Jesus' ministry according to regions, emphasizing his Galilean ministry. But his relationship with Mary, Martha, and Lazarus suggests that he had occasion to stay with them in Bethany on his way to Jerusalem. His secret friend, Joseph of Arimathea, seems to be from Jerusalem. And, John's Gospel depicts Jesus as a frequent visitor to the Garden of Gethsemane. In Matthew 23:37, Jesus speaks of longing to gather the people of Jerusalem as a hen gathers her chicks.

In prophetic fashion, Jesus' dramatic ride into Jerusalem demonstrated rather than described his messiahship. He declared himself a king of peace (the donkey-riding variety) rather than a white-stallion-riding, conquering king.

"God bless the one who comes in the name of the Lord!" from Psalm 118:26 can be translated as, "Blessed in the name of the Lord is the one who comes." "Hosanna!" is a simple transliteration of the Hebrew for "Save now!" The people were crying to Messiah Jesus to take the country back from their conquerors by force.

Though Jesus could have come to the Passover undercover and never been noticed, he chose to be public with his beliefs and teachings. Are we willing to do the same by announcing and standing up for our belief in God in a peaceful way?

Followers of Jesus give praise for Jesus.

Scope the

ZONE	TIME	SUPPLIES	⊚ ZONEZILLIES®
Zoom Into the Zone			
Get in the Zone	5 minutes	page 170, tape or safety pins, CD player	CD
Celebration Table	5 minutes	page 174, small table, white tablecloth, colored fabric, candle, Bible	inflatable palm tree
Make Palm Branches	10 minutes	Reproducible 2C on green construction paper, scissors	none
BibleZone®			
Gospel Talk	5 minutes	Bibles, Reproducible 2B (bottom), scissors	spiked rubber ball
Enjoy the Story	10 minutes	Reproducibles 2A–2B	none
Celebration Art	10 minutes	small bowls, water, tempera paint, dishwashing soap, paper, plastic spoons, plastic drinking straws, newspaper or old cookie sheets	none
Body Scramble	10 minutes	chalkboard, markerboard or large paper, chalk or marker, paper, markers	train whistle
LifeZone			
Praiseworthy Words	5 minutes	Reproducible 2D, pencils	none
Praise 'n Prayer	10 minutes	Reproducibles 1E and 2E, page 174, Celebration Table, CD player, palm branches	inflatable palm tree, CD

⊚ ZoneZillies® are found in the **BibleZone® LIVE FUNspirational® Kit.**

Zoom Into the Zone

Choose one or more activities to catch your children's interest.

Supplies:
page 170
tape or safety pins
CD player

ZoneZillies®:
CD

Get in the Zone

Play "Jesu, Jesu" **(CD)** as the students arrive. Greet each student with a happy smile.

Say: Welcome to BibleZone Live! I'm glad you are here. This is the fun place where we will get to know the Bible as our book!

If the students do not know one another, give them all nametags to wear (page 170).

Supplies:
page 174
small table
white tablecloth
colored fabric
candle
Bible

ZoneZillies®:
inflatable palm tree

Celebration Table

Ask one of the students who arrives early to help you prepare the Celebration Table. Cover the table and add a candle, a Bible, and colored fabric appropriate to the season, according to the instructions on page 12. For this session place the **inflatable palm tree** near the table.

Ask a student to prepare to read the closing prayer during your Praise 'n Prayer time. Give that student a copy of the prayer for week two (page 174).

Supplies:
Reproducible 2C (on green construction paper)
scissors

ZoneZillies®:
none

Make Palm Branches

Sometime before class begins, use green construction paper to make two copies of **Reproducible 2C** for each student.

Hand out two copies of Reproducible 2C and scissors for each student. Make sure that the students understand the directions. When the branches are complete, ask the students to place the palm branches near your Celebration Table. These will be used during your closing time.

24

Choose one or more activities to immerse your children in the Bible story.

Gospel Talk

Before class, photocopy and cut apart the Scripture cards (**Reproducible 2B, bottom**).

Hand out Bibles and divide the class into the following four groups: Matthew, Mark, Luke, and John. Ask the members of each group to find the book in the Bible that their group is named after.

Say: Today's story is found in all four Gospels: Matthew, Mark, Luke, and John. The story is about Jesus being greeted by the crowds as he rode into Jerusalem. We celebrate that day every year and call it Palm Sunday. I will hand you a piece of paper with the Scripture passages on it. Look up the passage for your group based on the name I gave your group and read it to see why we call that day Palm Sunday.

After they have read their Scriptures in their groups, ask a volunteer from each group to read their Scripture out loud. Initiate discussion by using the **spiked rubber ball** and the questions listed below.

Ask: What did you read in your assigned Scripture that might tell us why we call the day we celebrate Jesus' entrance into Jerusalem Palm Sunday? How were the Scriptures different? Why do you suppose there is a difference in the Scriptures?

Supplies:
Bibles
Reproducible 2B
   (bottom)
scissors

ZoneZillies®:
spiked rubber ball

Enjoy the Story

Hand out **Reproducibles 2A–2B**.

Ask for volunteers to read the story aloud. Remind the students that today's story is told from the perspective of a donkey.

Supplies:
Reproducibles 2A–2B

ZoneZillies®:

From the Donkey's Mouth

(based on Mark 11:1-11)

by Delia Halverson

I live a pretty simple life in a village just outside Jerusalem. My master provides me with plenty of food, and I always have a pile of straw to sleep on at night.

I earn my keep by helping my master carry the vegetables he has grown, the animals he has raised, and the bread and cheese his family has made to the marketplace in Jerusalem. But today my duties changed.

It all started early in the morning when the crowds began to pass through my village on the way to the Temple in Jerusalem. This is the week of Passover, and there are many pilgrims on their way to worship God at the Temple this week.

I awoke to tromping, scuffling feet and the sound of wheels grinding over rocks and sand on the road outside my stable. Some people were riding on animals or carts, but most of them were walking in sandals or bare feet covered with the dust of the many miles they had traveled.

About mid-morning, I was tied, as usual, beside the door of my master's house. As I waited to be loaded with the day's produce, two men came up to me and untied my rope.

While they were untying me, the people standing nearby asked, "Why are you untying the donkey?" It seemed like a logical question!

The men answered, "The Lord needs it and will soon bring it back." That was when I realized that I was in for a very unusual day!

The two men took me to a small group of men—their friends, I assumed—who seemed to be waiting for us. Several of the men took off their cloaks, snapped them in the air, and watched them float down onto my back to make a soft saddle.

A man with very kind eyes came up to me, rubbed my head, stroked my shoulders, talked to me in the way people who talk to donkeys generally talk, and then climbed on my back.

As we started down the road, crowds began to gather. There were parents, children, grandparents, and single folks. Everyone was shouting and singing! The kind man on my back and I seemed to be the center of attention.

Some people went into the nearby fields and cut branches that they laid across the road in front of us. Others took off their cloaks and laid them on the ground for me to walk on. That was certainly something different! I felt like the most honored donkey in the country!

Surely this had to be a king riding on my back! Who else would be greeted like this? The best part is that he didn't ride me into some kind of battle like many kings are known to do.

26

But I shouldn't have worried. No king would ever have ridden the likes of me off to war! I was an animal that only has value in times of peace, so I felt safe in assuming that his intentions were peaceful. If he had been riding into battle or to proclaim a victory, it would have been on the back of a horse.

This man seemed to place importance on those donkeys and persons who weren't usually believed to be important by others. He was the type of person who would say that the first shall be last and the last shall be first.

All in all, it was quite a day! The people along our route shouted, "Hooray! God bless the one who comes in the name of the Lord! God bless the coming kingdom of our ancestor David. Hooray for God in heaven above!"

Matthew 21:8-9	**Luke 19:36–38**
Mark 11:8–10	**John 12:12–13**

27

Celebrating Palm Sunday

When Jesus came into Jerusalem before his crucifixion,
the people crowded the streets waving palm branches
and shouting praises to God for Jesus. Carefully cut the palm branch
from the paper, being sure to cut between the fronds on the branch.

Reproducible 2C

BibleZone® LIVE

Bible

Choose one or more activities to immerse your children in the Bible story.

Celebration Art

Protect the tables with newspaper or place a cookie sheet under each small bowl. Put ten spoonfuls of tempera paint, one spoonful of dishwashing soap, and one spoonful of water in a small bowl. Stir until mixed. Make several colors using several different bowls. Give each student a plastic straw.

Say: We are going to make celebration pictures that praise God for Jesus. Put the straw into the paint mixture and blow gently, making bubbles. When the bubbles rise about an inch above the edge of the bowl, curl a piece of paper and gently touch the bubbles with it. Don't let the paper touch the rim of the bowl. Then lift the paper and see what designs the paint bubbles have made. The designs make a picture of joy. Allow that color to dry, and then you may add another color.

Supplies:
small bowls
water
dishwashing soap
paper
plastic spoons
plastic drinking straws
newspaper or old
   cookie sheets
tempera paint

ZoneZillies®:
none

Body Scramble

Write the Bible verse on a chalkboard, a markerboard, or a large sheet of paper. Assign one word plus the Scripture reference to thirteen students. If you have fewer than thirteen students, give some students two words, but give them words adjacent to each other in the sentence and have them write both words on the same paper.

Ask each student to write their word in large letters on an 8½- by 11-inch sheet of paper. Have those students stand in a random order holding their words where they cannot be seen. Then when you blow the **wooden train whistle**, have them hold their words in front of them and see how fast they can unscramble the words of the Bible verse to put them in order. Any students not holding a word can help verbally. When they have found their places, read the Bible verse together.

After doing this once, mix the papers up and hand them out again. Repeat the process and time the students. Continue as time allows, trying to arrange the placement faster each time. Repeat the Bible verse each time you unscramble the words. If you have more than thirteen students, give other students an opportunity to hold a word each time you scramble the words.

Supplies:
chalkboard, marker-
   board, or large
   paper
chalk or marker
paper
markers

ZoneZillies®:
train whistle

Supplies:
Reproducible 2D
pencils

ZoneZillies®:
none

Supplies:
Reproducibles 1E and
    2E
page 174
Celebration Table
CD player
palm branches made
    earlier

ZoneZillies®:
inflatable palm tree
CD

Praiseworthy Words

Hand out **Reproducible 2D** and pencils. Be sure that the students understand and follow the directions.

Praise 'n Prayer

Distribute copies of **Reproducible 1E** and play "The Servant Song" **(CD, Track 1)** to call the class to the Celebration Table for Praise 'n Prayer. Light the candle and call their attention to the appropriate seasonal color and the **inflatable palm tree** beside the table.

Ask: Why do you suppose we have a large palm tree beside our Celebration Table today?

Accept their suggestions.

Say: There are many different types of trees in the land where Jesus lived. Many of them are palm trees. Some of the writers who tell about Jesus' ride into Jerusalem do not say what type of branches were put in the road, but one does mention palm branches. It is likely that they used palm branches because there were so many palm trees in the area around Jerusalem. We will wave the palm branches that we made as we sing the chorus to our song.

Hand out **Reproducible 2E**, "Hosanna to the King!", and play the song **(CD, Track 2)**. Listen to the music first and then sing it together, waving the palm branches during the chorus.

Ask the student you assigned earlier to close with the following prayer (also on page 174): "Our God, we praise you, and we thank you for sending Jesus, the Messiah. Amen."

Make a copy of HomeZone® for each student in your class.

PRAISE BISCUITS

½ cup butter
1 three-ounce package cream cheese
2 cups flour
1 tablespoon baking powder
½ cup sugar
½ teaspoon salt
½ cup milk
orange marmalade

Set the butter and cream cheese out of the refrigerator 30 minutes before beginning the biscuits. Mix flour, baking powder, sugar, and salt in the bowl. Add butter and cream cheese and mix well with a pastry blender or two table knives. The mixture should be the size of small peas. Add the milk to the flour mixture and stir just enough to wet the dry ingredients well.

Roll out on a floured surface until the dough is a little less than ½ inch thick. Cut with a biscuit cutter or the lip of a glass. Dip the biscuit cutter or glass in flour after you cut each biscuit. Using kitchen scissors, make five small cuts evenly around the edge of each biscuit being careful not to cut all the way to the center. Place the biscuits onto a cookie sheet and press your thumb into the center of each biscuit to make a hole. Spoon ½ teaspoon of marmalade into the center of each biscuit.

Bake at 450 degrees for 10 to 12 minutes or until golden brown.

ThinkZone

Why is it important for me to praise God? What specific things do I see around me each day that I praise God for?

Praise Collage

Make a collage of different ways to praise God. At the top of a large piece of paper print, "We praise you, O God." Cut pictures from magazines that show ways that we can praise God and glue them on the page, overlapping the pictures so that the page is solid with pictures. Put the collage somewhere in your home where everyone can see it.

Memory Verse
God bless the one who comes in the name of the Lord!

Mark 11:9

Followers of Jesus give praise for Jesus.

Praise God

There are many words that we use and actions that we do when we praise God. Below is a list of some of those words and actions. Look for the words of praise diagonally, across, or up and down. Check the words off the list as you find and circle each one.

```
M  V  K  S  Y  J  O  Y  F  U  L
A  A  W  O  N  D  E  R  F  U  L
P  M  G  L  O  R  I  O  U  S  Q
D  H  A  N  E  S  P  A  H  O  E
E  O  H  R  I  A  G  R  E  A  T
S  S  H  P  V  F  P  P  Q  Z  E
S  A  D  V  R  E  I  Y  W  I  R
E  N  A  J  S  A  L  C  C  U  N
L  N  N  Y  I  H  I  O  E  P  A
B  A  C  E  N  I  I  S  U  N  L
V  A  E  H  G  O  R  N  E  S  T
```

Praise	Wonderful	Great	Hosanna
Sing	Joyful	Marvelous	Blessed
Dance	Glorious	Magnificent	Eternal

Reproducible 2D

BIBLEZONE® LIVE

Song Zone

Hosanna to the King!

Hosanna, Hosanna, Hosanna to the King!
Sing we in one accord.
Hosanna, Hosanna, Hosanna to the King!
Blessed is the one who comes in the name of the Lord.

The people of Jerusalem
welcomed their coming King.
They laid their cloaks down at his feet
as they began to sing:

Hosanna, Hosanna, Hosanna to the King!
Sing we in one accord.
Hosanna, Hosanna, Hosanna to the King!
Blessed is the one who comes in the name of the Lord.

While Jesus rode on a donkey's back,
he greeted the people there.
And those who came to see their Lord
waved palm branches in the air.

Hosanna, Hosanna, Hosanna to the King!
Sing we in one accord.
Hosanna, Hosanna, Hosanna to the King!
Blessed is the one who comes in the name of the Lord.

WORDS and MUSIC: Mark Burrows
© 2001 Abingdon Press, admin. by the Copyright Co., Nashville, TN

Jesus Serves

Enter the ZONE

Bible Verse
I have set the example.
John 13:15

Bible Story
John 13:1-20

Taking up the towel and basin, Jesus reinforced the message he had attempted to get through to his followers: In order to be great, one must serve others—sometimes in roles that demand humility.

Unpaved Palestinian roads would become several inches of dust in dry weather and mud during wet weather. With nothing more than simple sandals as footwear, feet were always dirty. So, houses had large pots of water at the door where a servant would wash and dry the feet of family and guests using a basin and a towel. Unable to afford the luxury of a servant, Jesus would have expected the disciples, in keeping with tradition, to wash the feet of their rabbi.

When his disciples seemed unwilling to attend to this menial job, Jesus took the task himself. He filled the basin with water, wrapped the towel around his waist, and knelt before each disciple to wash his feet.

Perhaps Peter was in shock as Jesus began washing his companions' feet, only coming to his senses as Jesus stooped to remove Peter's sandals. In response to Peter's protest, Jesus said that unless Peter accepted this service, he did not belong to Jesus. Fine, said Peter. Why stop there? If you're going to go that far to embarrass yourself and me, don't stop with my feet! Or perhaps Peter's response was, Lord, my feet are not the only part of my body that has come into contact with the world's filth. Wash all of me! Baptism had become the rite of entrance into the church before John's Gospel was written—complete with the symbolism of Christ's ultimate sacrifice for us and an appreciation for the power of the community formed around that sacrifice. While the washing of feet for entrance to home and for meals was all that was required, much like with the symbolic washing of baptism, a person thus admitted was expected to become the servant willing to do whatever might be required in order to extend hospitality and draw in the next person.

Followers of Jesus set an example for others.

Scope the

ZONE	TIME	SUPPLIES	⊚ ZONEZILLIES®
Zoom Into the Zone			
Get in the Zone	5 minutes	page 170, tape or safety pins, CD player	CD
Celebration Table	5 minutes	page 174, small table, white tablecloth, candle, basin and towel, Bible, colored fabric	none
BibleZone®			
Service Match	5 minutes	Reproducible 3C	click pen necklaces
Enjoy the Story	10 minutes	Reproducibles 3A–3B	spiked rubber ball
Puppets for Others	10 minutes	Reproducible 3D, pages 166 and 167, brown lunch-size paper bags, crayons, scissors, glue, CD player	CD
Follow the Servant Leader	10 minutes	index cards, marker, basket	none
LifeZone			
Praise 'n Prayer	10 minutes	Reproducibles 1E and 3E, page 174, Celebration Table, basin and towel, CD player	CD, spiked rubber ball

⊚ ZoneZillies® are found in the **BibleZone® LIVE FUNspirational® Kit.**

Zoom Into the Zone

Choose one or more activities to catch your children's interest.

Supplies:
page 170
tape or safety pins
CD player

ZoneZillies®:
CD

Get in the Zone

Play "Jesu, Jesu" **(CD)** as the students arrive. Greet each student with a happy smile.

Say: Welcome to BibleZone Live! I'm glad you are here. This is the fun place where we will get to know the Bible as our book!

If the students do not know one another, give them all nametags to wear (page 170).

Supplies:
page 174
small table
white tablecloth
colored fabric
candle
Bible
basin and towel

ZoneZillies®:
none

Celebration Table

Ask one of the students who arrives early to help you prepare the Celebration Table. Cover the table and add a candle, a Bible, and colored fabric appropriate to the season, according to the instructions on page 12.

For this session place a basin and towel beside the candle.

Ask a student to prepare to read the closing prayer during your Praise 'n Prayer time. Give that student a copy of the prayer for week three (page 174).

Choose one or more activities to immerse your children in the Bible story.

Service Match

Supplies:
Reproducible 3C

ZoneZillies®:
click pen necklaces

Hand out **Reproducible 3C** and the **click pen necklaces**. Be sure that the students understand the directions.

After the students have matched the pictures, collect the pens for another activity.

Enjoy the Story

Supplies:
Reproducibles 3A–3B

ZoneZillies®:
spiked rubber ball

Hand out **Reproducibles 3A–3B**. Assign persons to read the parts. Point out the parts that everyone will read together. Read the story together, and then use the **spiked rubber ball** to facilitate discussion.

Ask: People in that time walked dusty roads and wore sandals. Why do you suppose a servant did not wash his or her own feet when that servant came in? What do you suppose Jesus was trying to explain to the disciples when he washed their feet?

Puppets for Others

Supplies:
pages 166 and 167
Reproducible 3D
brown lunch-size
   paper bags
crayons
scissors
glue
CD player

ZoneZillies®:
CD

Ahead of time, make a sample puppet from **Reproducible 3D**, using the accessories on pages 166 and 167. Make plans to give the puppets to a preschool class or childcare facility.

Say: Jesus told us to find ways to serve others. We are going to make paper bag puppets that we can give to some younger children so that they can learn about people in our communities who serve others.

Hand out Reproducible 3D, pages 166 and 167, brown lunch-size paper bags, crayons, scissors, and glue. Show the students a sample of a puppet that you have made and have them begin working on their own puppets as you play "The Servant Song" **(CD)**, "Hosanna to the King!" **(CD)**, and "Jesu, Jesu" **(CD)** while they work.

Let the students choose the eyes, noses, mouths, and accessories they want to use to create their puppets. Praise each student's efforts.

Jesus Serves Friends

(based on John 13:1-20)

by Delia Halverson

Leader: It was before Passover, and Jesus knew that the time had come for him to leave this world and to return to the Father. He had always loved his followers in this world, and he loved them to the very end.

All: Jesus loved his disciples until the very end.

Leader: Even before the evening meal started, the devil had made Judas, the son of Simon Iscariot, decide to betray Jesus.

All: But Jesus continued to love *all* of his disciples until the very end.

Voice 1: Jesus knew that he had come from God and would go back to God.

Voice 2: He also knew that the Father had given him complete power.

Leader: So during the meal, Jesus got up and removed his outer garment then wrapped a towel around his waist. He put some water into a large bowl. Then he began washing his disciples' feet and drying them with the towel he was wearing.

Simon Peter: When he came to me, I asked, "Lord, are you going to wash my feet?"

Jesus: You don't really know what I am doing, but later you will understand.

Simon Peter: You will never wash my feet!

Jesus: If I don't wash you, you don't really belong to me.

Simon Peter: Lord, don't wash just my feet. Wash my hands and my head.

Jesus: People who have bathed and are clean all over need to wash just their feet. And you, my disciples, are clean, except for one of you.

Leader: Jesus knew who would betray him. That is why he said, "except for one of you." After Jesus had washed his disciples' feet and had put his outer garment back on, he sat down again.

Jesus: Do you understand what I have done?

All: Explain it, Lord.

Jesus: You call me your teacher and Lord, and you should, because that is who I am. And if your Lord and teacher has washed your feet, you should do the same for one another. I have set the example and you should do for one another exactly what I have done for you.

All: We should serve one another as Christ served us.

Reproducible 3A

BibleZone® LIVE

Jesus: I tell you for certain that servants are not greater than their master, and messengers are not greater than the one who sent them. You know these things and God will bless you if you do them.

All: We should serve one another as Christ served us.

Jesus: I am not talking about all of you. I know the ones I have chosen. But what the Scriptures say must come true.

Leader: The Scriptures say, "The man who ate with me has turned against me!"

Jesus: I am telling you this before it all happens. Then when it does happen, you will believe who I am.

All: We will know who Jesus is.

Jesus: I tell you for certain that anyone who welcomes my messengers also welcomes me, and anyone who welcomes me welcomes the one who sent me.

All: We welcome Christ, and we welcome God who sent him. Praise to God for Jesus Christ!

Service Match

Find the word that describes each act of service shown in
the pictures and write the correct word below each picture.
There are more words about service than there are pictures.
Choose the word that most closely matches the picture.

DONATE FOOD for the HUNGRY

TRASH

Painting

Helping

Reading

Caring

Feeding

Writing

Babysitting

Cleaning

Building

Teaching

Preaching

Reproducible 3C

BibleZone® LIVE

Choose one or more activities to immerse your children in the Bible story.

Follow the Servant Leader

This is game that is played like traditional "Follow the Leader." Each leader will draw a series of servant actions out of a basket. He or she will then do the action listed on the sheet while the players must mimic the actions and guess the serving action that is being portrayed. When a player guesses the action, then he or she becomes the leader and draws a new series of actions from the basket. Ahead of time, photocopy and cut apart the following series of actions on index cards with one series on each card, then place them in a basket.

Supplies:
index cards
marker
basket

ZoneZillies®:
none

Knock on a door, open the door, sit down, pick up and open a book, pretend to read. (*Reading to someone.*)

Pour the ingredients in a bowl, stir the ingredients, pour the contents into a pan, put the pan in oven, take the pan out of oven, give the prepared food to someone. (*Cook a meal for someone.*)

Knock on a door, open the door, smile, walk inside, pick up a pretend baby, rock the baby. (*Baby-sit.*)

Pick up a songbook, open to a page, play a piano, sing as you play, occasionally wave your hand as though directing others to sing. (*Sing and play in a nursing home.*)

Knock on a door, open the door, point to a wall, pull a paintbrush from pocket, dip brush into paint can, begin to paint imaginary wall. (*Paint someone's home.*)

Knock on a door, shake hands with someone, close the door, begin to rake the yard, plant flowers, mow the lawn. (*Care for someone's yard.*)

Knock on a door, take and read over a list, take money and put it in your pocket, walk to a grocery story, place food in a cart, check out, carry groceries back to the house. (*Do grocery shopping for someone.*)

Walk up to a door, unlock it, keep dog from jumping up on you, put a leash on the dog, take it outside for a walk, go back to the house, pour food and water into dishes and place them on the floor. (*Care for someone's dog.*)

Take a bucket off a shelf, fill it with water from a hose, take the bucket and hose to a car, hose the car off, wash car. (*Wash someone's car.*)

Supplies:
Reproducibles 1E and
   3E
page 174
Celebration Table
basin and towel
CD player

ZoneZillies®:
CD
spiked rubber ball

Praise 'n Prayer

Play and sing "The Servant Song" **(Reproducible 1E; CD, Track 1)** to call the class to the Celebration Table for Praise 'n Prayer. Light the candle and call their attention to the appropriate seasonal color and the basin and towel on the table.

Use the **spiked rubber ball** to initiate discussion about the following questions.

Ask: Why do you suppose we have a basin and towel on our Celebration Table? How do you think it would feel to have Jesus wash your feet? Why would we give praise for Jesus because he washed the disciples' feet?

Hand out **Reproducible 3E**, "Jesu, Jesu." Play through the song once **(CD)** and then sing it together.

Ask the student you assigned earlier to close with the following prayer (also on page 174): "Our God, we want to be servants for you. Help us to know how to help others. Amen."

Make a copy of HomeZone® for each student in your class.

BIRD BANQUET

Jesus told us to care for others. We must also care for animals. Make a bird banquet by tying a ribbon or cord to the top of a pine cone. This will be used to hang it on a tree or pole. Spread some peanut butter on the outside of the cone and some between the sections of the cone. Roll the cone in bird seed. Push double-pointed toothpicks into the pine cones and stick apple chunks on these toothpicks.

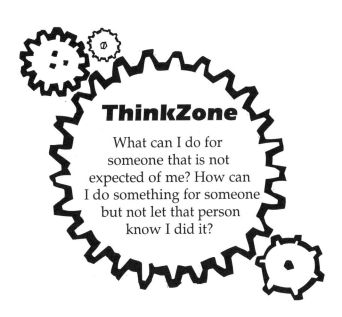

ThinkZone

What can I do for someone that is not expected of me? How can I do something for someone but not let that person know I did it?

Memory Verse
I have set the example.
John 13:15

Taco Dump Soup

This is a simple soup that you can make for your family or for someone who needs a meal. After you brown the meat and onions, you simply dump it together into a big pot and heat until it is bubbly.

1 pound ground beef or turkey
1 medium onion, peeled and diced
1 15-ounce can pinto beans, undrained
1 cup water
1 package dry taco seasoning
1 15-ounce can corn, drained
1 15-ounce can stewed tomatoes
1 15-ounce can kidney beans, undrained

You may add grated cheese to the top as you serve it.

Followers of Jesus set an example for others.

Reproducible 3D

Permission granted to photocopy for local church use. © 2005 Abingdon Press.

BibleZone® LIVE

Jesu, Jesu

Jesu, Jesu, fill us with your love,
show us how to serve the neighbors we have from you.

Kneels at the feet of his friends,
silently washes their feet,
Master who acts as a slave to them.

Jesu, Jesu, fill us with your love,
show us how to serve the neighbors we have from you.

Neighbors are rich and poor,
varied in color and race,
neighbors are near and far away.

Jesu, Jesu, fill us with your love,
show us how to serve the neighbors we have from you.

These are the ones we should serve,
these are the ones we should love,
all these are neighbors to us and you.

Jesu, Jesu, fill us with your love,
show us how to serve the neighbors we have from you.

Loving puts us on our knees,
serving as though we are slaves,
this is the way we should live with you.

Jesu, Jesu, fill us with your love,
show us how to serve the neighbors we have from you.

Kneel at the feet of our friends,
silently washing their feet,
this is the way we should live with you.

Jesu, Jesu, fill us with your love,
show us how to serve the neighbors we have from you.

WORDS: Tom Colvin
MUSIC: Ghana folk song; arr. by Tom Colvin; harm. by Charles H. Webb
© 1969 and 1989 Hope Publishing Co.

The Saddest Day

Enter the *ZONE*

Bible Verse

God did not keep back his own Son, but he gave him for us.

Romans 8:32

Bible Story

Luke 22:39-53, 66-71; 23:1-5, 13-25

To contend with all that awaited him, Jesus prepared himself with prayer. He immersed himself in the awareness of God's presence so that he would be able to allow the chain of events that had been initiated to continue to its conclusion. Jesus knew that a cross was the "reward" for opposition to Roman authority and that his challenge to religious authority would be made to look like a threat to Rome and would be used to seal his destiny.

"Jesus was in great pain and prayed so sincerely that his sweat fell to the ground like drops of blood" (Luke 22:44). The Greek word for "great pain" means "agony" or the sheer fear of an intense battle. Jesus could have lost himself in the Passover crowds. No doubt many anticipated or hoped that he would do so. But to avoid the cross meant denying his beliefs and his identity. Jesus clung to whom he was and to what God desired.

Having prayed, Jesus came to his disciples, his betrayer, and his captors in peace. He brought healing and peace when a disciple attempted to defend him by drawing a sword and cutting off the ear of the high priest's servant. Surrendered to God's will, he faced life and death with absolute serenity and perfect confidence in God's ultimate victory.

The verdict of blasphemy handed down by the Sanhedrin was never mentioned as Jesus was brought before the Roman governor. In a matter of hours, the charge of blasphemy, which the Romans would have laughed at, evolved into "inciting a riot," "encouraging people to evade taxes," and "claiming to be a king." Neither Pilate nor Herod found any substantiation for the charges brought against him. Pilate called upon the tradition of releasing a Jewish prisoner at Passover as cause to release Jesus, but the people were determined to silence Jesus—even at the cost of releasing a known criminal back onto the streets and nailing one who was no criminal to a cross.

Followers of Jesus stand up for what they believe.

Scope the

ZONE	TIME	SUPPLIES	⊚ ZONEZILLIES®
Zoom Into the Zone			
Get in the Zone	5 minutes	page 170, tape or safety pins, CD player	CD
Celebration Table	5 minutes	page 174, small table, white tablecloth, colored fabric, candle, Bible, piece of wood that shows growth circles (optional: Reproducible 4D)	none
Creed Crossword	5 minutes	Reproducible 4C, pencils	none
BibleZone®			
Speedy Search	10 minutes	Reproducible 4B, bookmarks, Bibles, scissors, envelopes	train whistle
Enjoy the Story	10 minutes	overhead projector, Transparency 1, Reproducibles 4A–4B optional: biblical costume, shower curtain or sheet, erasable markers	spiked rubber ball
Tree of Faith	10 minutes	Reproducible 4D, overhead projector, Transparency 2, transparency marker	click pen necklaces
LifeZone			
Praise 'n Prayer	10 minutes	Reproducible 4E, piece of wood, Celebration Table, page 174, CD player	CD

⊚ ZoneZillies® are found in the **BibleZone® LIVE FUNspirational® Kit.**

Zoom Into the Zone

Choose one or more activities to catch your children's interest.

Supplies:
page 170
tape or safety pins
CD player

ZoneZillies®:
CD

Get in the Zone

Play "Jesu, Jesu" **(CD)** as the students arrive. Greet each student with a happy smile. If the students do not know one another, give them all nametags to wear (page 170).

Say: Welcome to BibleZone Live! I'm glad you are here. This is the fun place where we will get to know the Bible as our book!

Supplies:
page 174
small table
white tablecloth
colored fabric
candle
Bible
wood piece
optional: Reproducible 4D

ZoneZillies®:
none

Celebration Table

Ask one of the students who arrives early to help you prepare the Celebration Table. Cover the table and add a candle, a Bible, and colored fabric appropriate to the season, according to the instructions on page 12.

For this session place a piece of wood that shows growth circles on it or a copy of **Reproducible 4D** beside the candle.

Ask a student to prepare to read the closing prayer during your Praise 'n Prayer time. Give that student a copy of the prayer for week four (page 174).

Supplies:
Reproducible 4C
pencils

ZoneZillies®:
none

Creed Crossword

Hand out **Reproducible 4C** and pencils. Read the information at the top together first, and then allow the students to work together in teams to fill out the crossword. Be sure that they also fill in the blanks in the creed.

Answers:
1. *created*
2. *love*
3. *worship*
4. *human*
5. *died*
6. *guides*
7. *believe*
8. *welcome*
9. *family*
10. *Bible*
11. *help*
12. *love*

Choose one or more activities to immerse your children in the Bible story.

Speedy Search

Hand out Bibles and divide the students into teams of two or three.

Say: Find Romans 8:32 and read it as many times as you can. When I blow the train whistle, **put the bookmark in the place and close the Bible. You have two minutes.**

Give each team an envelope containing the Bible verse cards you have reproduced, cut apart, and mixed up **(Reproducible 4B, right)**. Have all the students close their Bibles and work cooperatively to put the verse in the correct order.

Supplies:
Bibles
bookmarks
Reproducible 4B
envelopes
scissors

ZoneZillies®:
wooden train whistle

Enjoy the Story

Turn on the overhead projector and project **Transparency 1** on the wall. The black-and-white transparency may be colored using erasable markers. If you project the image on the back of a plain shower curtain or sheet, you may sit in front without disturbing the scene.

Ask the students to sit together on the floor at the base of the projected transparency and pretend to be a disciple in their minds during the story. You may dress in biblical costume, if you like, and take the position of the owner of the garden as you tell or read the story on **Reproducibles 4A–4B**. Afterwards, give a copy of the reproducible to each student.

After the story use the **spiked rubber ball** to initiate discussion based on the questions listed below.

Ask: When you pretended to be a disciple, how did you feel about what was being told? How did you feel about the way that Jesus stood up for being able to say what he believed? What might you have done if you had been there?

Supplies:
Reproducibles 4A–4B
Transparency 1
overhead projector
optional: biblical
   costume, plain
   shower curtain or
   sheet, erasable
   markers

ZoneZillies®:
spiked rubber ball

The Saddest Day

(based on Luke 22:39-53, 66-71; 23:1-5, 13-25)

by Delia Halverson

Welcome to the Mount of Olives. Look at this garden all around you. It's beautiful, isn't it? I'm the owner of this garden, and I invited Jesus to use the garden any time he liked. It became one of his favorite places to be close to God.

On the last evening he spent with his disciples—the night he was arrested—this was where he came. In fact, it was here that his enemies found him. They took him off for a trial that really wasn't a true trial and then had him put to death—a real death.

Of course we know the end of the story, but those disciples that night did not know that Jesus would be raised from the dead. Imagine yourself in the place of one of the disciples as I tell you the story.

After Jesus had eaten the Passover meal with his disciples, he came to this garden. He told them, "Pray that you won't be tested," and then he went a little distance and knelt down and prayed, "Father, if you will, please don't make me suffer by having me drink from this cup. But do what you want, and not what I want."

You see, Jesus could have lost himself in the masses of people who had come to Jerusalem for the Passover. But if he had, he would never have been able to speak out for what he believed again. Jesus was struggling with what God wanted him to do. In fact, the disciples say that he was struggling so much that sweat fell to the ground like drops of blood.

The disciples also told me that they were so tired that they fell asleep, and Jesus found them sleeping. When he woke them up, a crowd began to gather and they recognized Judas among them. Judas had left the dinner early and now he was back with many of the chief priests, Temple police, and other leaders. He greeted Jesus with a kiss, but Jesus knew what was going on and said, "Are you betraying the Son of Man with a kiss?"

The disciples realized that Jesus was about to be arrested, and one of them asked, "Lord, should we attack them with a sword?" In fact, one of them did strike at the servant of the high priest and cut his right ear off. Jesus said, "Enough of that!" and he healed his ear.

Then Jesus spoke to those who came to arrest him and said, "Why do you

Reproducible 4A

come out with swords and clubs and treat me like a criminal? I was with you every day in the Temple and you didn't arrest me."

Then they took Jesus with them, and at day-break they brought him before their religious council and accused him of saying he was the Messiah. Jesus simply answered, "If I said so, you wouldn't believe me. And if I asked you a question, you wouldn't answer. But from now on, the Son of Man will be seated at the right side of God." Even when they asked him if he is the Son of God he just said, "You say I am!"

Next, they took him to Pilate, who was the government head of the Romans at the time. There they changed their charge against him. They knew that Pilate didn't care if Jesus claimed to be God, but Pilate did care about avoiding riots, so they said, "We caught this man trying to get the people to riot and to stop paying taxes to the emperor. He also claims that he is our king."

Pilate asked him, "Are you the king of the Jews?"

And in Jesus' usual manner of turning things around, he said, "Those are your words."

The Roman government usually releases a prisoner during the Passover and Pilate asked the crowd if he should release Jesus or the well-known murderer Barabbas. But the crowd had gotten so riled up that they chose Barabbas and wanted Jesus killed. They kept yelling, "Nail him to a cross! Nail him to a cross!"

And so Jesus was taken away and nailed to the cross. There would be no more praying in my garden. It was the saddest day that I can remember.

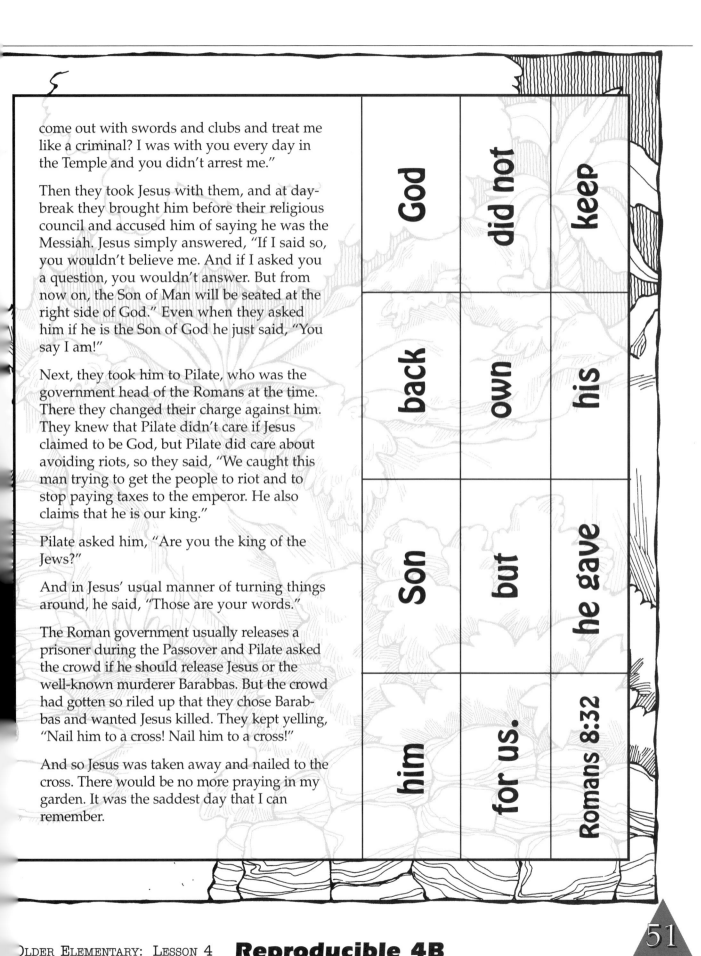

God	did not	keep
back	own	his
Son	but	he gave
him	for us.	Romans 8:32

This We Believe

A statement of our belief is called a creed. This creed was written by the confirmation class of Northbrook United Methodist Church in Roswell, Georgia. Find the missing words in the puzzle and then read the creed. Do you believe what the class said they believe?

We believe in God, the almighty Father, who is the one supreme God who (1) _ _ _ _ _ _ _ the heavens, the earth, and everything in between.

We believe God is here, there, and everywhere.

We believe we should try to be a mirror of God and a reflection of God's (2) _ _ _ _ to people around us.

We believe God's word is true and we should show our thanks to God through praise, prayer, song, and (3) _ _ _ _ _ _ _ _.

We believe in Jesus!

We believe that Jesus Christ is our Savior, God's firstborn son sent to earth in (4) _ _ _ _ _ form.

We believe Jesus is a part of the Holy Trinity.

We believe that while on earth Jesus taught, healed and saved.

We believe Jesus (5) _ _ _ _ for us to heal our sins and bless the whole world.

We believe in the Holy Spirit.

We believe the Holy Spirit is the third part of the Trinity.

We believe the Holy Spirit empowers us, (6) _ _ _ _ _ _ us, comforts us, encourages us, strengthens us, and finds us.

We (7) _ _ _ _ _ _ _ _ the Holy Spirit lives inside each one of us.

We believe in the Church.

The church is a place that everyone is (8) _ _ _ _ _ _ _ and treated equally.

The church is a place to praise and worship God, and a place to hang out and make friends.

The church is God's (9) _ _ _ _ _ _ that comes together to help others.

We promise to have faith in the Holy Trinity, to be kind to others, to read the (10) _ _ _ _ _, and to have a good attitude.

We promise to not break the Ten Commandments, to be committed to church, to make time for God, and to pray.

We promise to (11) _ _ _ _ those in need,

to listen, to support, to respect, to honor, to (12) _ _ _ _, to trust one another, and to forgive. Amen.

52

Reproducible 4C

BibleZone® LIVE

Choose one or more activities to immerse your children in the Bible story.

Tree of Faith

Hand out **Reproducible 4D** and the **click pen necklaces**. Project **Transparency 2** on the wall. Read the information at the top of the reproducible. If you have time during this activity, have some students share their thoughts.

Say: Close your eyes and think of a time when you felt very warm—physically or emotionally. It might have been a time you felt very loved. Now think of a time in worship that was meaningful. Now think of a time you helped someone and knew that it was what God wanted you to do. Maybe it was a mission project or something you did on your own.

Write "Experienced Faith" on the center circle of the transparency and ask them to write it on their reproducible at the same place.

Say: The times you just thought of were part of your experienced faith. Next, think of people who have helped you understand God in some way. It might be someone at church or a parent or friend.

After a moment, write "Affiliated Faith" on the next circle on the transparency. Ask them to write it on their reproducible at the same place.

Say: The word _affiliated_ has to do with the people you connect with, your friends, and the people around you. This is another part of your faith. Think about something you once believed about God or God's world that you don't believe now. Maybe you thought thunder was the result of angels bowling in heaven or that God would zap you if you did something wrong.

After a moment, write "Questioning Faith" on the next circle on the transparency. Ask them to write it on their reproducible in the corresponding place.

Say: Questioning our faith occurs when we think about ideas or things we've been told about God and we ask ourselves if that is what we believe. Some people are afraid to question what they've been told to believe, but if we really think about it, this thought and questioning process only makes our belief even stronger. Don't be afraid to ask questions and to think about your beliefs. Even adults ask questions and continue to think about what they believe. Sometimes adults even change their minds about beliefs after thinking about them for a while.

Supplies:
Reproducible 4D
Transparency 2
overhead projector
transparency marker

ZoneZillies®:
click pen necklaces

Choose one or more activities to bring the Bible to life.

Write "Owned Faith" on the outer circle of the transparency and ask them to do the same.

Say: When you have done a lot of study about the Bible and about God, when you've spent time listening to God, and when you've spent time following what God wants, you will add the fourth type of faith, "Owned Faith."

Supplies:

Reproducible 4E
Celebration Table
page 174
CD player
piece of wood that
    shows growth
    circles

ZoneZillies®:

CD

Praise 'n Prayer

Play and sing "The Servant Song" **(CD)** to call the class to the Celebration Table for Praise 'n Prayer.

Light the candle and call their attention to the appropriate seasonal color and the cross section of the tree on the table.

Say: Why do you suppose we have a cross section of a tree on our Celebration Table? Remember how we talked about the different circles of faith? The circles in a tree remind us of that.

Hand out **Reproducible 4E**, "Were You There?" Play the song once **(CD)** and then sing it together.

Ask the student you assigned earlier to close with the following prayer (also on page 174): "Our God, we want to learn more about you and to know your presence every moment of our lives. Help us to be like Jesus, growing in faith and standing up for what we believe. Amen."

Make a copy of HomeZone® for each student in your class.

My CREED

A creed is a statement of what you believe. Create your own creed by completing the following sentences:

I believe in a God who . . .
I believe that Jesus . . .
I believe that the Holy Spirit is . . .
I believe that the church exists to . . .
I believe that God wants me to . . .

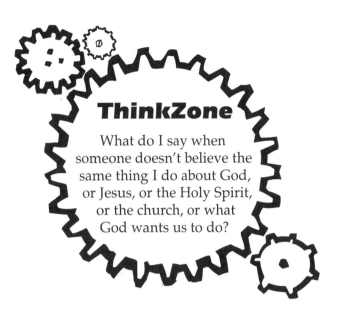

ThinkZone

What do I say when someone doesn't believe the same thing I do about God, or Jesus, or the Holy Spirit, or the church, or what God wants us to do?

Memory Verse

God did not keep back his own Son, but he gave him for us.

Romans 8:32

Pizza Twists

1 package of eight refrigerated bread sticks
½ cup spaghetti or pizza sauce
8 ounces shredded mozzarella cheese
finely chopped black olives (optional)

Unroll the breadsticks and place them on a flat dish or plate. Use a pastry brush to brush about a tablespoon of spaghetti or pizza sauce over half of each breadstick. Put about one ounce of mozzarella cheese over the sauce. Add a few pieces of black olives (if desired). Fold the plain half of the bread stick over the sauce-covered half and twist it to seal the edges.

Place the pizza twists on a lightly greased baking sheet and bake at 350 degrees for 15–20 minutes, until lightly browned.

Followers of Jesus stand up for what they believe.

The Way We Understand God

The way we understand God and become closer to God is something
like the way a tree grows. Each year a tree adds another ring of growth,
but it does not throw away the old rings. Each ring of the tree
helps the tree all through its life.

56

Reproducible 4D

BibleZone® LIVE

Were You There?

Were you there when they crucified my Lord?
Were you there when they crucified my Lord?
Oh sometimes it causes me to tremble, tremble, tremble.
Were you there when they crucified my Lord?

Were you there when they nailed him to the tree?
Were you there when they nailed him to the tree?
Oh sometimes it causes me to tremble, tremble, tremble.
Were you there when they nailed him to the tree?

Were you there when they laid him in the tomb?
Were you there when they laid him in the tomb?
Oh sometimes it causes me to tremble, tremble, tremble.
Were you there when they laid him in the tomb?

WORDS: African American spiritual
MUSIC: African American spiritual; adapt. and arr. by William Farley Smith
Adapt. and arr. © 1989 The United Methodist Publishing House

OLDER ELEMENTARY: LESSON 4 **Reproducible 4E**

Out of the Tomb

Enter the

Bible Verse

Only you are God! And your power alone, so great and fearsome, is worthy of praise.

Psalm 99:3

Bible Story

Matthew 28:1-10

Though each Gospel writer tells the story of Easter morning differently, each recalls that women were the first to arrive at the empty tomb. John writes that Mary Magdalene came alone, while Matthew has her accompanied by another Mary. Mark and Luke recall several women. Matthew is the only one to report that the women witnessed the stone's removal by the angels.

In Matthew the women do not come to anoint the body of Jesus, as is remembered by Mark and Luke, but they simply come to see and to be close to Jesus—to dare to draw close to his dead body. It was risky to appear too curious about someone who was crucified, since contact with the dead rendered one ceremonially unclean. Perhaps Jesus' claim that he would be raised in three days brought them to the tomb to see if it was true. Having witnessed the death and burial, they came with the hope of Resurrection.

The reality of the empty tomb was such a staggering discovery that an angel had to urge the women to believe that it was for real. Remember that angels represent the presence of God, which means that it was the women's awareness of the very presence of God at the empty tomb that convinced them that Jesus was alive, just as he had predicted, though this realization stood in stark contrast to all that they had seen.

As the women left the tomb, Jesus himself met them and assured them that it was indeed true, and urged them to tell the disciples and have them meet him in Galilee.

Christ's call challenges us to respond with three actions: to believe, even when belief appears completely irrational; to tell others what we have come to believe, regardless of how we think they may react; and to rejoice in our relationship with God by following Christ's command. We would not know about the depth of God's love if others before us had not accepted this challenge. Now it is our turn.

Scope the

ZONE	TIME	SUPPLIES	⊚ ZONEZILLIES®
Zoom Into the Zone			
Get in the Zone	5 minutes	page 170, CD player, tape or safety pins	CD
Celebration Table	5 minutes	page 174, small table, white tablecloth, colored fabric, dry bulb or onion, candle, Bible	none
An Awesome God	5 minutes	Reproducible 5C, crayons	click pen necklaces, spiked rubber ball
BibleZone®			
Fearsome Findings	5 minutes	Bibles	spiked rubber ball
Enjoy the Story	10 minutes	Reproducibles 5A–5B	spiked rubber ball
Easter Candles	10 minutes	beeswax sheets, candle wicks, baking sheet, wax paper, skillet of warm water, ruler, small plastic flowers, scissors	none
Growth by an Awesome God	5 minutes	Reproducible 5D	tape measure key chains, click pen necklaces
LifeZone			
Praise 'n Prayer	10 minutes	Reproducible 5E, Celebration Table, page 174, dry bulb or onion, CD player	spiked rubber ball, CD

⊚ ZoneZillies® are found in the **BibleZone® LIVE FUNspirational® Kit.**

Zoom Into the Zone

Choose one or more activities to catch your children's interest.

Supplies:
page 170
CD player
tape or safety pins

ZoneZillies®:
CD

Get in the Zone

Play "Hallelujah Chorus" **(CD)** as the students arrive. Greet each student with a happy smile.

Say: Welcome to BibleZone Live! I'm glad you are here. This is the fun place where we will get to know the Bible as our book!

If the students do not know one another, give them all nametags to wear (page 170).

Supplies:
page 174
small table
white tablecloth
colored fabric
candle
Bible
dry bulb or onion

ZoneZillies®:
none

Celebration Table

Ask one of the students who arrives early to help you prepare the Celebration Table. Cover the table and add a candle, a Bible, and colored fabric appropriate to the season, according to the instructions on page 12.

For this session place a dry bulb or an onion beside the candle.

Ask a student to prepare to read the closing prayer during your Praise 'n Prayer time. Give that student a copy of the prayer for week five (page 174).

Supplies:
Reproducible 5C
crayons

ZoneZillies®:
click pen necklaces
spiked rubber ball

An Awesome God

Hand out **Reproducible 5C, click pen necklaces**, and crayons. After the students have completed the page, read the Zone-In phrase together. Then use the **spiked rubber ball** to initiate discussion.

Ask: What do you consider to be evidence of the awesomeness of God? (Examples are *Creation, beauty, magnificence seen in nature, the performance of kind acts by people we believe to be inspired by God, and so forth. If no one suggests it, mention God raising Jesus from the dead as the work of an awesome God.*)

60

Choose one or more activities to immerse your children in the Bible story.

Fearsome Findings

Supplies:
Bibles

ZoneZillies®:
spiked rubber ball

Have a variety of Bible translations on hand, including the Contemporary English Version. Hand out the Bibles and ask the students to turn to and read Psalm 99:3 silently. Next, have them take turns reading the verse aloud from the translation they have. Point out the word *fearsome* (CEV) and ask if anyone knows what the word means.

Say: The ending "some" means that what is being described causes or is capable of causing the first part of the word. "Burdensome" describes something that places a burden on someone. "Worrisome" describes something that causes worry. "Troublesome" describes something that causes trouble. "Fearsome" describes something capable of causing fear, but the Bible does not necessarily use this to mean scary. Something fearsome frightens us because it is so different from us, so strange or unknown, or because we have never experienced it. Other translations use the word *awesome*—**capable of causing awe.**

Ask someone to read the verse using the word *awesome* in the place of *fearsome*. Invite the students to give examples of people, things, or experiences that they consider awesome. Use the **spiked rubber ball** to facilitate their discussion.

Enjoy the Story

Supplies:
Reproducibles 5A–5B

ZoneZillies®:
spiked rubber ball

Hand out **Reproducibles 5A–5B** and have the students take turns reading the story with each one reading a portion. After reading, discuss the story using the **spiked rubber ball** so that everyone has a turn speaking.

Ask: Imagine that you are one of the Roman soldiers guarding Jesus' tomb. How do you think you might have felt when Jesus' resurrection happened? How would you explain this to your supervisors? How might your supervisors react? How does this story reflect God's awesomeness?

Report of
the Roman Guard

(based on Matthew 28:1-10)

by Delia Halverson

Duty station: <u>Outside Jerusalem, tomb of Jesus of Nazareth, crucified Friday.</u>

Time of duty:<u> Sunday, midnight to just after dawn.</u>

Condition of site upon arrival: <u>No one in vicinity. Stone covering tomb already set in place over entrance, tomb sealed with Pilate's seal. All quiet. Area secured.</u>

Incidents during guard duty (describe in detail):

Just before dawn we heard quiet voices and saw two women approaching the tomb. We thought it strange that the women should come so early and alone, but we did not see them as a security risk and let them approach. What followed is difficult to describe, but I will attempt to do so.

Without any warning, an earthquake shook the ground. When we were able to stand we went to make sure that the women were not hurt and observed what we can only describe—although none of us is religious—as an angel descending from heaven! No human being could have moved that stone alone, but this being did just that and then sat on the stone as though the stone had just been conquered! This being was bright as lightning with clothes as white as snow. I confess that we were so afraid that we shook like the earthquake was creating aftershocks, and we all collapsed to the ground like dead men.

Reproducible 5A

Then that being, the angel, spoke to the women saying, "Don't be afraid! I know you are looking for Jesus, who was nailed to a cross. He isn't here! God has raised him to life, just as Jesus said he would."

Like us, the women were in shock and the angel invited them to see the place where the body had been lying, then to go and tell his disciples that he has been raised to life and was on his way to Galilee. The angel said, "Go there, and you will see him. That is what I came to tell you."

The women seemed to recover faster then we did. With a strange mixture of fear and joy in their faces, they ran from the tomb, presumably to do as the angel had directed. As the women were leaving, a man came out of nowhere and greeted them. It was obvious that they knew him because they fell at his feet and worshiped him. The man said, "Don't be afraid! Tell my followers to go to Galilee. They will see me there."

Condition of area at the end duty: <u>The seal was broken and the tomb was empty.</u>
<u>These were very strange and startling events!</u>

Signature of Reporting Officer: *Lucius Placidus Scato*

Color the Picture

Use the symbol key below to color this picture.
What does the Resurrection say about God?

= red   = blue   ✝ = green   = yellow   = brown

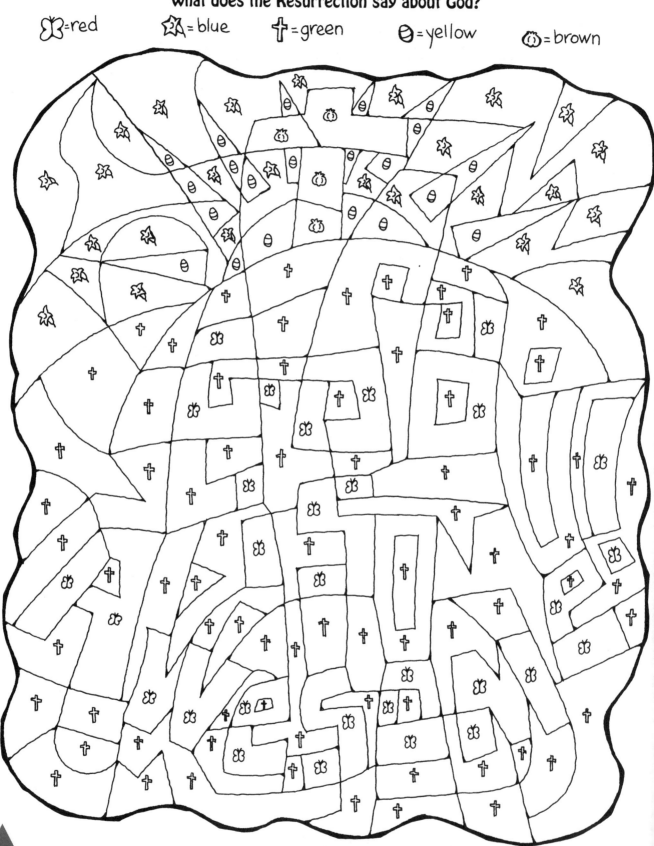

Reproducible 5C

BibleZone® LIVE

Choose one or more activities to immerse your children in the Bible story.

Easter Candles

Purchase sheets of beeswax and candle wicks at a hobby store. Cut the sheets into square pieces. You can usually get two candles from one sheet.

Warm the sheets by laying them on a baking sheet that has been covered with wax paper and placing the baking sheet over a skillet of lukewarm water. Beeswax melts quickly, so watch that it does not get too warm.

Place a ruler one-half inch from one edge and turn the edge up to form a groove for the wick. Insert a wick that is at least one inch longer than the candle.

Begin rolling the beeswax. On the last roll press the edges so that the wax melts into the body of the candle. While the candle is still warm, press plastic flowers into the sides of the candle. Trim the bottom of the candle to make it flat and even. The top can be trimmed at a slant.

Supplies:
beeswax sheets
candle wicks
baking sheet
wax paper
skillet of warm water
ruler
small plastic flowers
scissors

ZoneZillies®:
none

Growth by an Awesome God

Ask the students if any of them know what their length was at birth. Tell them that an average baby is about eighteen or nineteen inches at birth. Pass out the **tape measure key chains** and have them measure the amount of inches they were at birth, or eighteen inches if they don't know their birth statistics, to get an idea of how small they were at birth. If they were born prematurely, they may have been much smaller.

Hand out **Reproducible 5D** and the **click pen necklaces**. Help them take measurements and fill in the blanks. As you work, talk about how our growth and our mental development is a part of how awesome God is.

Supplies:
Reproducible 5D

ZoneZillies®:
tape measure key
  chains
click pen necklaces

Life ZONE

Choose one or more activities to bring the Bible to life.

Supplies:
Reproducible 5E
Celebration Table
page 174
dry bulb or onion
CD player

ZoneZillies®:
spiked rubber ball
CD

Praise 'n Prayer

Play "The Servant Song" **(CD)** to call the class to the Celebration Table for Praise 'n Prayer. Light the candle and call their attention to the appropriate seasonal color and the dry bulb or onion on the table. Pick up the dry bulb or onion and use the **spiked rubber ball** to initiate discussion.

Ask: Do you think this is dead or alive? If you had never seen it grow into a plant, would you think it could produce a flower? (*Remember that even an onion puts out a flower. Remind them that the Easter lilies that we use to celebrate Easter were at one time like this dried-up bulb*). **How does this dried-up bulb remind you of our story?** (*Something that appears dead comes to life*). **What does our story and this bulb say about God's power?** (*Read the Zone-In phrase and then ask them to repeat it with you several times: "Followers of Jesus know that God's power is awesome!" Ask if they can suggest other things that show us the awesome power of God, such as the power of a waterfall, the wind, our brains, the growth of a giant tree from an acorn or seed, the ability to heal that God has given doctors, and so forth*).

Hand out **Reproducible 5E**, "Hallelujah Chorus," and play the song **(CD)** while the students follow along. Review the Easter story as told by the song and then sing the song together.

Ask the student you assigned earlier to close with the following prayer (also on page 174): "Our God, forgive us for those times when we understand you as being anything less than awesome. Help us to see your awesomeness in everything around us. Fill us with awe as we consider how you raised Jesus from death. Amen."

Make a copy of HomeZone® for each student in your class.

CARROT CAKE

2 cups flour
2 cups sugar (you can use light brown sugar)
2 tsp soda
1 tsp salt
2 tsp cinnamon

Mix dry ingredients listed above and add:
1½ cups cooking oil
4 eggs

Mix and add:
3 cups grated raw carrots (about 6 medium carrots)
½ cup nuts

Pour into a greased 9- by 13-inch pan and bake at 350 degrees for 35–40 minutes.

Icing: (If you prefer, cut this recipe in half)
8 oz. cream cheese
4 cups powdered sugar, sifted
1 stick butter
2 tsp. vanilla

ThinkZone

Where do I see God's awesome power today? How can I remember to look for God in my life every day?

Memory Verse

Only you are God! And your power alone, so great and fearsome, is worthy of praise.

Psalm 99:3

New Crayons

Recycle crayons by making them into new shapes. You will need old crayons, foil cupcake wrappers, resealable plastic bags, and a wooden mallet or cloth-covered hammer.

Peel the wrappers off crayons of similar colors and place them in a plastic bag. Squeeze as much air as possible out of the bag and gently break up the crayon pieces with the mallet or hammer. Smaller pieces melt more quickly.

Fill a foil cupcake wrapper about three-quarters full with crayon pieces and place the filled cupcake wrapper in the hot sun to melt. You can also place it on a foil-covered baking sheet and put it in the oven at 250 degrees for a few minutes to melt. If you use the oven, watch closely so it doesn't overheat.

Let the new crayon cool until hard. Then pop it out of the foil wrapper. Use spring colors to make a gift for a young child.

Followers of Jesus know that God's power is awesome!

Awesome Growth Chart

_____ (name), a child of God.

I have been growing ____ years.

Weight at birth _____

Weight today _____

Length at birth _____

Height today _____

At birth my arms were not very long.
Today my arm is _____ inches long.

At birth my feet were so small that both of them could fit in an adult's hand.
Today my feet are _____ inches long.

At birth, here are some of the things I could do:
_____
_____
_____

By the time I entered school here are some of the things I could do:
_____
_____
_____

Today I have grown enough that I can do these things:
_____
_____
_____

God gives us growth. My God is an awesome God!

Only you are God!
And your power alone,
so great and (awesome),
is worthy of praise.
(Psalm 99:3, adapted)

Reproducible 5D

BibleZone® LIVE

Song

Hallelujah Chorus

"Hallelujah! Hallelujah!"
Everybody stand and say,
"Hallelujah! Hallelujah!"
Jesus rose on Easter Day!

When the Marys saw the tomb,
their eyes were opened wide.
An angel sent down by the Lord
had rolled the stone aside.

"Hallelujah! Hallelujah!"
Everybody stand and say,
"Hallelujah! Hallelujah!"
Jesus rose on Easter Day!

"Do not fear," the angel said,
"But go to Galilee;
for there you'll find the risen Christ;
a joy for all to see."

"Hallelujah! Hallelujah!"
Everybody stand and say,
"Hallelujah! Hallelujah!"
Jesus rose on Easter Day!

As they ran to Galilee,
they met Christ on the way.
He wanted them to tell the news
about this joyous day.

"Hallelujah! Hallelujah!"
Everybody stand and say,
"Hallelujah! Hallelujah!"
Jesus rose on Easter Day!

WORDS: Mark Burrows
MUSIC: Mark Burrows
© 2002 Abingdon Press, admin. by The Copyright Co., Nashville, TN 37212

The Emmaus Road

Enter the ZONE

Bible Verse

All of us can tell you that God has raised Jesus to life!

Acts 2:32

Bible Story

Luke 24:13-35

Using the formula of the suspense story, this tale tells the readers the identity of the mysterious figure on the road to Emmaus, but the other characters in the story have to figure it out for themselves. We want to shout at the two disciples, "What is wrong with you? Can't you see who this is?" Grief was what was wrong with them—a grief so consuming that they couldn't see any reality beyond their own sense of loss.

Jesus could have said, "Come on now, don't you recognize me?" Instead, he allowed them the healing grace of telling their story one more time. He then shifted into his rabbi/teacher role and responded to the sense of finality and hopelessness that these disciples had expressed by setting their experience in the context of God's will.

Was it just a sense of hospitality that prompted the two to invite Jesus to stay with them in Emmaus, or was it the realization of their need for the comfort that his words provided? In either case, he accepted the invitation and was soon offering a

blessing as they sat down to break bread and share a meal together. As they received the broken bread, they suddenly realized who he was, and then just as suddenly, Jesus was gone.

Jesus did not force himself upon these disciples. Instead, he made himself available to them and allowed them to draw their own conclusions. The two men on the road to Emmaus definitely knew that they were missing something. But though they believed they were missing Jesus himself, they came to realize that it was their confidence in the Resurrection that was actually missing—a confidence that the stranger on the road began to restore.

Though it took on a sacramental nature, this act of breaking bread was an ordinary meal in an ordinary home, reminding us that mind-boggling truths like the Resurrection can often come to us in the midst of the routine and the ordinary—in the church, in the classroom, and beyond.

Followers of Jesus know that Jesus is alive!

Scope the

ZONE	TIME	SUPPLIES	⊚ ZONEZILLIES®
Zoom Into the Zone			
Get in the Zone	5 minutes	page 170, CD player, tape or safety pins	CD
Celebration Table	5 minutes	page 174, small table, white tablecloth, colored fabric, candle, Bible, unsliced loaf of bread	none
BibleZone®			
Seek and Find Code	5 minutes	Reproducible 6D, pencils, Bibles	none
Enjoy the Story	5 minutes	Reproducibles 6A–6B	none
Prayer "Tent" Cards	10 minutes	Reproducible 6C, construction paper, scissors, glue, crayons or markers	none
May I Join You?	10 minutes	page 173, bag or basket, scissors	train whistle
LifeZone			
Praise 'n Prayer	10 minutes	Reproducible 6E, Celebration Table, page 174, loaf of bread, CD player	CD

⊚ ZoneZillies® are found in the **BibleZone® LIVE FUNspirational® Kit.**

Zoom Into the ZONE

Choose one or more activities to catch your children's interest.

Supplies:

page 170
CD player
tape or safety pins

ZoneZillies®:

CD

Get in the Zone

Play "Hallelujah Chorus" **(CD)** as the students arrive. Greet each student with a happy smile.

Say: Welcome to BibleZone Live! I'm glad you are here. This is the fun place where we will get to know the Bible as our book!

If the students do not know one another, give them all nametags to wear (page 170).

Supplies:

page 174
small table
white tablecloth
colored fabric
candle
Bible
unsliced loaf of
  bread

ZoneZillies®:

Celebration Table

Ask one of the students who arrives early to help you prepare the Celebration Table. Cover the table and add a candle, a Bible, and colored fabric appropriate to the season, according to the instructions on page 12.

For this session place an unsliced loaf of bread beside the candle.

Ask a student to prepare to read the closing prayer in your Praise 'n Prayer Time. Give that student a copy of the prayer for week six (page 174).

72

 Bible Z⊙NE®

Choose one or more activities to immerse your children in the Bible story.

Seek and Find Code

Hand out **Reproducible 6D**, Bibles, and pencils. Be sure that the students understand the directions. The answer is today's Bible verse.

Supplies:
Reproducible 6D
pencils
Bibles

ZoneZillies®:
none

Enjoy the Story

Hand out **Reproducibles 6A–6B** and assign parts (The Road, Cleopas, Friend, and Stranger). Let the students enjoy the story.

Supplies:
Reproducibles 6A–6B

ZoneZillies®:
none

Prayer "Tent" Cards

Hand out **Reproducible 6C**, construction paper, scissors, glue, and crayons or markers. Create tent cards by using the prayers on Reproducible 6C. These will be taken home to be used on their tables at mealtimes.

Cut the prayers apart. Each prayer will be used on one "tent" of paper. The size of the prayer will determine the size of the construction paper. Fold the construction paper in half to form "tents" that will stand alone. Glue a prayer on one side and decorate both sides appropriately with crayons or markers.

As you work, talk about how Jesus broke bread with the two men that he met on the road to Emmaus. Remind the students that each time we pray before meals, we are following Jesus' example of thanking God for our food.

Supplies:
Reproducible 6C
construction paper
scissors
glue
crayons or markers

ZoneZillies®:

Men on the Road

(based on Luke 24:13-35)

by Delia Halverson

Road: I am a Roman road, a path of rocks, sand, gravel, and sun-baked soil that is crushed and packed down by passing feet, hooves, and wheels. Meandering around obstacles, I stretch the seven miles from Jerusalem to Emmaus. Or perhaps I should say from Emmaus to Jerusalem, since most everyone goes to Jerusalem and very few to the village of Emmaus.

Road: Passover travel has increased the amount of traffic taking advantage of me. All of the adult Hebrew males within walking distance were to be in Jerusalem unless age or health prevented them from making the trip. Emmaus, just a day's journey from Jerusalem, pretty much cleared out. Some, but not all, of the women went. They're not required to make all of the pilgrimages and to keep all of the rituals because they are expected to care for the children and keep the house. I don't know why it's that way, but it is. Maybe someday it will change and the women can be a part of worship, just like the men. At any rate, my dust has been flying with so many traveling over me. When it finally settles, we'll see if anything is left!

Road: I'm guessing that the festival must be over because most of the people have returned. Two of the last to return were Cleopas and his friend. They live in Emmaus and travel my way fairly often. Just the two of them walked to Jerusalem, but a third man met up with them—kind of mysteriously—as they returned. I'm not sure exactly when he joined them. He was just there all of a sudden.

Road: Since I stretch the whole distance, I get to listen to entire conversations—long conversations as people travel along. Some of the pilgrims who returned right after the Passover talked about a crucifixion there on Friday, a man named Jesus. Crosses aren't exactly newsworthy in this part of the world. It's how Rome deals with those who threaten the *Pax Romana*—the "Roman Peace." From what Cleopas and his companions were saying, this particular cross was anything but ordinary.

Stranger: What were you talking about as you walked along?

Cleopas: Are you the only person in Jerusalem who didn't know what was happening there these last few days?

Stranger: What do you mean?

Cleopas: Those things that happened to Jesus from Nazareth. By what he did and said, he showed that he was a powerful prophet who pleased God and all the people.

Friend: Then the chief priests and our leaders had him arrested and sentenced to die on a cross.

74

Cleopas: We had hoped that he would be the one to set Israel free! But it has already been three days since all this happened.

Friend: Some women in our groups surprised us. They had gone to the tomb early this morning, but did not find the body of Jesus. They came back saying that they had seen a vision of an angel who told them that he was alive.

Cleopas: Some men from our group went to the tomb and found it just as the women had said. But they didn't see Jesus either.

Stranger: Why can't you understand? How can you be so slow to believe all that the prophets said? Didn't you know that the Messiah would have to suffer before he was given his glory? It's all written in the Scriptures. I will explain it to you, beginning with the Laws of Moses and the Books of the Prophets.

Road: The sun was going down at that point and the men were nearing Emmaus.

The stranger looked like he was going on, but Cleopas and his friend begged him to stay with them, so the stranger continued with them into the village. Inside the house they sat down to eat and the stranger lifted up the bread, blessed it, handed it to the men, and was gone! No, he didn't get up and leave. He disappeared!

Cleopas: When he talked with us along the road and explained the Scriptures to us, didn't it warm our hearts?

Friend: Why didn't we recognize the Lord until he broke the bread? We need to get back to Jerusalem and tell the others!

Road: So they are on their way now. It's too late to be traveling, but I don't think that is going to slow them down. Perhaps when they get back to Jerusalem they will find others who have seen this mysterious stranger as well.

I pray, dear God, that I may always recognize you in all that surrounds me.

You are an awesome God and I praise you forever. Amen.

My God,
On this day that is special
I pray for those less fortunate than I.
On this day that is special
I ask that you show me what I can do for others.
On this day that is special
I give what I have to you.
Amen.

Show me your ways,
O God,
and teach me to follow.
Guide me by your truth
and instruct me
in your way.
I trust that you will
always be with me.
Amen.

THANK YOU, GOD,
FOR SENDING JESUS.
THANK YOU FOR ALL THAT HE
TAUGHT WHILE HERE ON EARTH.
THANK YOU THAT JESUS IS ALIVE
AND ABLE TO HELP US TODAY.
THANK YOU FOR THOSE WHO LIVED
BEFORE ME AND KEPT
THE GOOD NEWS ALIVE.
AMEN.

FOR FOOD AND DRINK
I THANK YOU, GOD.
FOR ALL THAT BRINGS
ME JOY I THANK YOU,
GOD.
FOR THE HARD TIMES
I THANK YOU, GOD.
THROUGH THOSE
HARD TIMES I WILL
GROW.
MAKE ME FOREVER
THANKFUL.
AMEN.

As the sun shines, my God,
Help me to remember
that your light
shows me the way.
As the stars and moon
shine at night,
help me to remember
that you guide me
in dark times.
You are my guide
and my salvation.
Amen.

76

Reproducible 6C

Choose one or more activities to immerse your children in the Bible story.

May I Join You?

Ask the students to recall times they have invited someone to join them in a meal. Remind them that in our story the two men invited Jesus to spend the night with them and to share a meal.

Ask: How did you feel when the person you invited accepted the invitation? Once someone has accepted an invitation to a meal, what is required of us?

Play a game that is played similarly to "Captain, May I?" Choose someone to be "It." Copy the instructions on page 173 and cut them apart. Place the instruction slips in a bag or basket for "It" to use.

Mark a beginning line ("Jerusalem") and an ending line ("Emmaus") with masking tape on the floor. "It" stands at the ending line. Line everyone else up on the beginning line and have "It" draw an instruction from the bag, call a person's name, and read that instruction. The person called must ask, "May I join you?" "It" should answer, "Yes, you may" before the person called can move.

After each person follows the instruction, the whole class will respond in a shout with the Bible verse: "All of us can tell you that God has raised Jesus to life!"

Use a timer and in a given time blow the **train whistle** and have "It" trade places with someone else from the class. Continue changing the persons acting as "It" until everyone has moved to the finish line. Encourage the students to shout the phrase louder as the game comes to a close.

Supplies:
page 173
bag or basket
scissors
masking tape

ZoneZillies®:
train whistle

Choose one or more activities to bring the Bible to life.

Supplies:
Reproducible 6E
Celebration Table
page 174
loaf of bread
CD player

ZoneZillies®:
CD

Praise 'n Prayer

Play "The Servant Song" **(CD)** to call the class to the Celebration Table for Praise 'n Prayer. Light the candle and call their attention to the appropriate seasonal color.

Hand out **Reproducible 6E**, "We Remember You" **(CD)**. Sing the song together.

Hold the loaf of bread from the table and ask the students to stand in a semi-circle in front of the Celebration Table.

Ask: How does this loaf of bread remind you of our story this week?

The students may suggest that the bread reminds them of Communion. Acknowledge all answers and remind them that the men who met Jesus on the road to Emmaus recognized Jesus when he broke bread at the meal. Break the bread and have the students pass it from person to person. As each person takes a piece of the bread, the whole group will say, "Followers of Jesus know that Jesus is alive!"

Ask the student you assigned earlier to close with the following prayer (also on page 174): "Our God, we thank you that we are followers of Jesus and that we know that Jesus is alive. Amen."

Make a copy of HomeZone® for each student in your class.

78

SOAP CARVING

Get permission from an adult before doing this. If you have never used a knife, you will need to have guidance from an adult.

Select a rectangular bar of soap. Cut off any design that may be on the soap so that you have a smooth surface. Use a ball-point pen or other pointed object to draw a cross on the top of the soap. Cut off the corners of the soap and slowly cut away unwanted areas until you are down to the basic cross design. You will have to cut in both angles to make the corners where the cross bar meets the upright. Round off the edges of the cross by carefully scraping them away, smoothing the cross as you work. After you have finished the basic shape of the cross you may use a pointed object to draw a design on the cross.

ThinkZone

What makes me happy about the resurrection of Jesus? How can I share that happiness with others?

Orange Slush

2½ cups water
2 cups sugar
12-ounce can frozen orange juice concentrate
12-ounce can frozen lemonade
Lemon-lime or citrus flavored soda

Mix the water and sugar in a saucepan and simmer for twenty minutes. Add the orange juice and lemonade and stir well. Place in a plastic container and freeze.

When you are ready to serve, let the mixture thaw to a slushy state. Mix one part of the orange mixture to one part soda. You may add ice if you like.

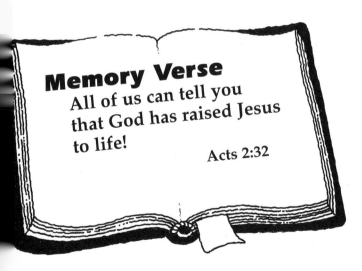

Memory Verse

All of us can tell you that God has raised Jesus to life!

Acts 2:32

Followers of Jesus know that Jesus is alive!

Seek and Find Bible Verse

Use the math code below to find the number to use for each letter in the words of the Bible verse. Then write the letters that match the numbers in the blanks.

‾‾‾ ‾‾‾ ‾‾‾   ‾‾‾ ‾‾‾   ‾‾‾ ‾‾‾   ‾‾‾ ‾‾‾ ‾‾‾
18   83   83   61   60   95   11   22   18   44

‾‾‾ ‾‾‾ ‾‾‾ ‾‾‾   ‾‾‾ ‾‾‾ ‾‾‾   ‾‾‾ ‾‾‾ ‾‾‾ ‾‾‾   ‾‾‾ ‾‾‾ ‾‾‾
99   20   83   83   62   61   95   99   58   18   99   50   61   16

‾‾‾ ‾‾‾ ‾‾‾   ‾‾‾ ‾‾‾ ‾‾‾ ‾‾‾ ‾‾‾ ‾‾‾   ‾‾‾ ‾‾‾ ‾‾‾ ‾‾‾ ‾‾‾
58   18   11   54   18   32   11   20   16   13   20   11   95   11

‾‾‾ ‾‾‾   ‾‾‾ ‾‾‾ ‾‾‾ ‾‾‾ !
99   61   83   32   60   20

Check your answer in Acts 2:32.

Code for letters:

A	$15 + 3 =$		L	$75 + 8 =$
C	$17 + 8 - 3 =$		N	$97 - 53 =$
D	$9 + 5 + 2 =$		O	$75 - 14 =$
E	$5 \times 4 =$		R	$18 \times 3 =$
F	$15 \times 4 =$		S	$7 + 4 =$
G	$25 \times 2 =$		T	$87 + 12 =$
H	$97 - 39 =$		U	$81 + 14 =$
I	$9 + 23 =$		Y	$49 + 13 =$
J	$7 + 6 =$			

Reproducible 6D

BibleZone® LIVE

We Remember You

We remember you,
Lord, we remember you.
When we break the bread,
when we take the cup,
we remember you.

We remember the time you broke the bread
and gave it to all your friends.
And today, when we break the bread,
we know your love for us never ends.

We remember you,
Lord, we remember you.
When we break the bread,
when we take the cup,
we remember you.

We remember the time you blessed the cup
and shared it with everyone.
And today, when we take the cup,
we know that you are God's special son.

We remember you,
Lord, we remember you.
When we break the bread,
when we take the cup,
we remember you.

WORDS and MUSIC: Mark Burrows
© 2002 Abingdon Press, admin. by The Copyright Co., Nashville, TN 37212

Two by Two

Enter the ZONE

Bible Verse
For we are partners, working together for God.
1 Corinthians 3:9a, Good News Translation

Bible Story
Mark 6:7-13

Since ancient Jews forbade the creation of "idols (images) that look like anything in the sky or on earth or in the ocean under the earth" (Exodus 20:4), we must depend on information about travel attire provided in wall paintings and sculptures created by other peoples of that period and region (see Reproducibles 7B and 7C). Seemingly minor details, along with insight about first-century travel, help us better understand Jesus' words as he sent out his disciples.

In verses 8 and 9 Jesus commanded the pairs of disciples to carry nothing extra. The idea of traveling light conveys a sense of urgency and the need for the disciples to cover as much territory as possible with their message and ministry. The traveling bag may refer to a wallet in which the traveler carried enough food for a day or two, but it could also refer to the "begging bags" used by priests and devotees of Greek gods and goddesses to collect food given as an offering to a certain deity. Perhaps Jesus was telling them that unlike the begging

priests, they were to be giving and not getting. Jesus clearly wanted the disciples to keep moving, to live simply, to trust God for everything, to focus on caring for others, and to call forth the best from persons by trusting in their sense of hospitality.

Travelers, as well as civilization as a whole, depended upon hospitality for survival. If a city failed to demonstrate an open spirit of kindness, generosity, and safety to strangers, sharing the gospel of Christ would have been fruitless; and the time of the disciples would have been better used in a more welcoming site. Shaking dust from one's feet signified that a relationship was not possible there.

Have you had people try to force their beliefs on you or attempt to purchase your acceptance of those beliefs? Jesus' disciples were not to operate this way. When the winsome story they carried met with a gracious welcome, miracles followed.

Followers of Jesus
tell others about Jesus.

Scope the

ZONE	TIME	SUPPLIES	⊚ ZONEZILLIES®
Zoom Into the Zone			
Get in the Zone	5 minutes	page 170, CD player, tape or safety pins	CD
Celebration Table	5 minutes	page 174, small table, white tablecloth, colored fabric, candle, Bible, sandals	none
On the Road	5 minutes	Reproducible 7D	click pen necklaces, spiked rubber ball
BibleZone®			
Enjoy the Story	10 minutes	Reproducible 7A	none
Rock Painting	10 minutes	rocks, newspapers, paint, paintbrushes, water and rags, chalkboard and chalk or large piece of paper and marker (optional: polyurethane spray)	none
Travel the Rocky Road	10 minutes	Transparency 3, overhead projector, Reproducibles 7B and 7C, self-adhesive notes (optional: permanent markers)	bouncing rock balls
LifeZone			
Praise 'n Prayer	10 minutes	Reproducible 7E, page 174, sandals, Celebration Table, CD player	spiked rubber ball, CD

⊚ ZoneZillies® are found in the **BibleZone® LIVE FUNspirational® Kit.**

Zoom Into the Zone

Choose one or more activities to catch your children's interest.

Supplies:
page 170
CD player
tape or safety pins

ZoneZillies®:
CD

Get in the Zone

Play "Hallelujah Chorus" **(CD)** as the students arrive. Greet each student with a happy smile. If the students do not know one another, give them all nametags to wear (page 170).

Say: Welcome to BibleZone Live! I'm glad you are here. This is the fun place where we will get to know the Bible as our book!

Supplies:
page 174
small table
white tablecloth
colored fabric
candle
Bible
sandals

ZoneZillies®:
none

Celebration Table

Ask one of the students who arrives early to help you prepare the Celebration Table. Cover the table and add a candle, a Bible, and colored fabric appropriate to the season, according to the instructions on page 12. For this session place a pair of simple sandals beside the candle.

Ask a student to prepare to read the closing prayer during your Praise 'n Prayer time. Give that student a copy of the prayer for week seven (page 174).

Supplies:
Reproducible 7D

ZoneZillies®:
click pen necklaces
spiked rubber ball

On the Road

Hand out **Reproducible 7D** and the **click pen necklaces**. Be sure that the students understand the instructions. After they have completed the puzzle, use the **spiked rubber ball** to encourage them to share the additional items that they listed at the bottom of the page.

Say: When we travel today, we take a great number of things with us. Jesus sent his friends out to tell others about God and told them to travel simply. Our story today reminds us of the instructions he gave to his followers.

Answers:
Across: 1. suitcase; 3. map; 6. sneakers; 8. ball; 9. books.
Down: 1. swimsuit; 2. game; 4. sandwich; 5. sodas; 7. jacket.

84

Choose one or more activities to immerse your children in the Bible story.

Enjoy the Story

Supplies:
Reproducible 7A

ZoneZillies®:
none

Ask: Can anyone tell me what the word *apostle* **means?** (*If no one can answer, explain that the word refers to one who is commissioned or sent out in ministry, such as a delegate, ambassador, or representative.*) **By contrast, a disciple is a student. Our word** *disciple* **comes from the Latin** *discipulus***, which means "student." Jesus the teacher called persons to follow and learn from him—to be his students or disciples. His closest twelve disciples are later referred to as "apostles" because they were sent out as Jesus' representatives to give leadership to the growing fellowship of believers. After Jesus' death, others selected as leaders of the early church, such as Paul, were also called "apostles."**

Hand out **Reproducible 7A**. You may read the leader part and assign someone to read the part of Jesus, or you may also assign the leader part. The response echoes today's ZoneIn®.

Rock Painting

Supplies:
clean rocks
paint
paintbrushes
newspapers
water and rags for
   clean-up
chalkboard and chalk,
   or large piece of
   paper and marker
optional:
   polyurethane spray

ZoneZillies®:
none

Ahead of time, clean rocks that are large enough for painting—one rock per student. Protect the tables with newspapers and lay the rocks out on a table, along with painting supplies.

Say: Remember that the roads in Jesus' time were very rocky. When Jesus sent the apostles out, they were traveling on those rocky roads. We are going to paint rocks to remind us of just what Jesus told us about God. What are some words that tell us about God?

Write the suggestions on a chalkboard or a large piece of paper. Then have the students choose their rocks and paint them as they wish, including a word that tells about God on each one. Remind them that the rocks will help them think about what Jesus told us. If you want to protect the rocks so that they can be used outside in a garden, cover the rocks with two or more coats of polyurethane spray.

Two by Two

(based on Mark 6:7-13)

by Delia Halverson

Leader: Jesus called his apostles together and sent them out two by two to spread the message.

Jesus: You may take along a walking stick, for the way will be rocky and long.

All: From Jesus we learn about God. He sends us to tell this to others.

Jesus: Travel light—leave behind extra food, a traveling bag, or money.

All: From Jesus we learn about God. He sends us to tell this to others.

Jesus: Wear sandals, for the road will be dusty and hot, but don't bother with a change of clothing.

All: From Jesus we learn about God. He sends us to tell this to others.

Jesus: When welcomed into a home with hospitality, stay there until you leave that town. There you will find folks who listen.

All: From Jesus we learn about God. He sends us to tell this to others.

Jesus: When you find you're not welcome, when people won't listen, leave and shake the dust of that town from your feet as a warning to them. Leave their resistance behind and move on.

All: From Jesus we learn about God. He sends us to tell this to others.

Leader: The apostles, the sent ones, departed by twos and told all the people they met, "Turn to God." Even today Jesus sends us all out to tell others the things that we've learned about God.

All: From Jesus we learn about God. He sends us to tell this to others.

Reproducible 7A

BibleZone® LIVE

Clothing for the Rocky Road

1. In biblical times people wore clothing that protected them from the sun. We do not have actual clothes that have survived all these years, but we have wall paintings and sculptures that show the clothing. The Hebrews were not allowed to create images of people, and so most of the paintings and sculptures we have from that era come from other countries.

2. Women usually washed the clothing when needed, pounding the dirt out of the wet clothing on flat stones and using soap made from olive oil. They did not have enough clothing to change frequently. The average person probably had only one set of clothing, while richer people had additional clothing.

3. Men wore a simple loincloth beneath their clothing. When their work required it, they took off their other clothing and wore only the loincloth.

4. Both men and women wore a simple, loose tunic. This was usually made from one piece of fabric, sewn together on one side. This garment reached almost to the feet. Two holes were cut into the tunic for the arms. Occasionally a tunic might have tight-fitting sleeves. If a tunic was made for sale, the hole for the head was not cut before the sale. This proved that it was a new tunic, and it also allowed the person to cut the head hole according to his or her needs. The neckline for men and women differed, since women who had to nurse their babies needed lower necklines.

5. The outer garment, or the cloak, was used when warmer clothing was needed. It was used as a coat in the daytime and as a blanket at night. This was made of a long piece of wool folded and sewn down the back to make a square with holes for the arms. Sometimes the cloak was woven in a manner that required no seams.

6. A belt or girdle was worn around the tunic and cloak. The skirts of the tunic could be tucked up under the belt for working or running. The tunic could also be tucked into the belt in a manner to form a pocket for carrying a package, or to form a money pocket.

7. In the heat of that country it was important to keep the head covered, protecting it from direct sunlight. They used a piece of fabric about a yard square, and it was folded diagonally and placed so that the long end of the triangle covered the neck. It also protected the cheeks and eyes. The head dress was held in place by a long piece of wool cloth. The wool would stretch to provide a comfortable fitting.

8. Sandals were the foot gear. The were flat soles of leather, wood, or matted grass. The edges of the sandals had loops for a strap that wrapped around the foot to keep the sandal on the foot

9. Travelers usually had a traveling bag, sometimes called a wallet. This was made of the skin of a young goat. Sometimes the animal was skinned whole, leaving it in the shape of the animal with the legs, tail, and head still attached. A strap was attached to each end so that it could be carried over the shoulder.

10. When a man entered the Temple, he was to put aside his staff and remove his shoes and money belt. He did this out of respect for the holiness of the Temple.

11. When a traveler entered a city, it was the duty of those living there to offer hospitality. The traveler did not have to try to find things that would satisfy his or her needs; these things were to be automatically offered to visitors. A lack of hospitality indicated a lack on interest in what the traveler had to say.

12. If a Hebrew traveled outside the country to the neighboring country of a non-believer or Gentile, upon reentering the country he or she was to shake the dust of the other country off his or her feet.

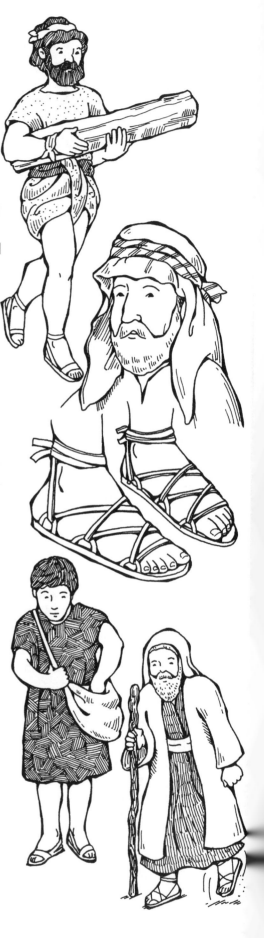

Reproducible 7C

BibleZone® LIVE

Choose one or more activities to immerse your children in the Bible story.

Travel the Rocky Road

Supplies:
Transparency 3
overhead projector
Reproducibles 7B and
   7C
self-adhesive notes
optional: permanent
   markers

ZoneZillies®:
bouncing rock balls

Transparency 3 will be used with this game. The black-and-white transparency may be colored using permanent markers.

Hand out **Reproducibles 7B** and **7C**. Put Transparency 3 on the overhead projector and project it on the wall.

Ask the students to line up according to their birthdays, starting with today. (If you have more than twelve students, select one from each month so that there are twelve players. The others will be cheerleaders or may be the ones to read the information.)

In turn, each student will take a **bouncing rock ball** and throw it at one of the rocks on the overhead. When the rock is hit, the player will read the information on the reproducible with that number.

After reading the information, mark that rock with a piece of self-adhesive paper (from a notepad) so that you know that it has been hit and cannot be thrown at again.

After all of the rocks have been hit, ask how the information makes a difference in understanding the story.

Choose one or more activities to bring the Bible to life.

Supplies:
Reproducible 7E
page 174
sandals
Celebration Table
CD player

ZoneZillies®:
spiked rubber ball
CD

Praise 'n Prayer

Play "The Servant Song" **(CD)** to call the class to the Celebration Table for Praise 'n Prayer. Light the candle and call attention to the appropriate seasonal color and the sandals on the table.

Ask: Why do you suppose we have a pair of sandals on our Celebration Table? (*The sandals remind us that Jesus not only sent people out to spread the good word about God in his time on earth, but he also sends us out to tell others about God.*)

Use the **spiked rubber ball** for discussion.

Ask: What is one way that you can tell others about Jesus this week? Each of you think of one way and share it with the group.

Hand out **Reproducible 7E**, "The Summons" **(CD)**. Play the song through once while the students follow and then sing it together.

Ask the student you assigned earlier to close with the following prayer (also on page 174): "Our God, we thank you for those whom Jesus sent out to tell others about you. Help us to share what we have learned with others. Amen."

Make a copy of HomeZone® for each student in your class.

90

Memory Verse

For we are partners,
working together for God.
1 Corinthians 3:9a,
Good News Translation

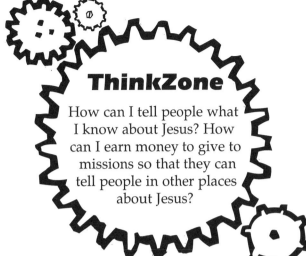

ThinkZone

How can I tell people what I know about Jesus? How can I earn money to give to missions so that they can tell people in other places about Jesus?

Missions Bank

You will need: a small metal container with a removable plastic lid (such as those from nuts or specialty coffees or teas); colored construction paper; clear, vinyl, self-adhesive paper; colored markers; scissors; clear tape; and glue.

Collect information about mission projects or specific missionaries supported by your church and select one that you would like to support. Gather the materials needed for the bank.

Cut a piece of construction paper to fit around the container, leaving a little extra so that the ends will overlap. Cut a piece of clear, vinyl, self-adhesive paper the same size. Glue the paper to the side of the container to cover the original label. Using markers or pieces of construction paper and glue, create a picture on the container that represents the mission project you have chosen. Remove the backing from the clear adhesive paper and cover the picture you've created on the container to protect it and make it last longer. With the scissors, carefully cut a slot in the plastic lid large enough so that money can be inserted, but not so large that the money would come out easily.

Have your family help you come up with a fun way to fill the container with your missions donations. For example, on Mondays put a penny in for every clothing article that you put in the clothes hamper over the weekend. Put in two pennies for those that didn't make it to the hamper but should have. On Tuesdays add a penny for each time you go in or out of the door to your home. Once the container is full, take it to church and make sure that the persons who handle such donations know where you want the money to go.

Followers of Jesus
tell others about Jesus.

Going on a Trip

Across:

1. You would use a __ __ __ __ __ __ __ __ to pack your clothing in.

3. You would take a __ __ __ so that you could know where you are going.

6. You might take extra __ __ __ __ __ __ __ __ to wear on your feet.

8. You might take a __ __ __ __ to play with at your destination.

9. You might pack some __ __ __ __ __ to read on your trip.

Down:

1. You might take a __ __ __ __ __ __ __ __ to wear if you were going to the beach.

2. You might take a __ __ __ __ to entertain yourself in the car.

4. You might take a __ __ __ __ __ __ __ for when you get hungry.

5. You might take __ __ __ __ __ for when you get thirsty.

7. You might take a __ __ __ __ __ __ __ to keep you warm if you were going to the mountains.

What additional things might you take on your trip?

Reproducible 7D

BibleZone® LIVE

The Summons

Will you come and follow me
If I but call your name?
Will you go where you don't know
and never be the same?
Will you let my love be shown,
will you let my name be known,
will you let my life be grown
in you and you in me?

Lord, your summons echoes true
when you but call my name.
Let me turn and follow you
and never be the same.
In your company I'll go
where your love and footsteps show.
Thus I'll move and live and grow
in you and you in me.

WORDS: John Bell
MUSIC: Traditional Scottish
Words © 1987 WGRG The Iona Community (Scotland), admin. by GIA Publications Inc.

Ten Lepers

Enter the Zone

Bible Verse
Your faith has made you well.
Luke 17:19

Bible Story
Luke 17:11-19

The road Jesus traveled from Galilee to Judea and Jerusalem took him a bit closer to Samaria than most Jews were inclined to go. Luke, always a champion of the underdog, positioned this story on the border where persons with leprosy might be found, pushed to the margins of both Galilean and Samaritan society where there was a reduced risk of coming in contact with the healthy or the presumably righteous.

The ten lepers stood at a distance, as they had been taught and as their culture demanded, and were most likely identifiable from far off by their chant of "unclean, unclean." But recognizing Jesus as the one who was reputed to have brazenly associated with the unclean and reversed what was believed to be evidence of God's curse, they dispensed with the chant long enough to shout out, "Jesus, Master, have pity on us!"

Since only a priest had the authority to diagnose the disease and to declare a person cured, Jesus looked in their direction and shouted back, "Go show yourselves to the priests." Jesus had no need to get closer and examine the size and color of the rash or lesions, which is what the priest would have done. Jesus was being Jesus. His role was Healer. Let the priests do what priests do. But as the lepers walked away, they were healed. When one of them became aware of the healing, he turned back, shouting praise to God for his restored flesh. Because his healing was so obvious, he dared to throw himself at Jesus' feet and offer him thanks. Then comes the clincher: this particular leper was a Samaritan! The other nine, healed but ungrateful, were presumably non-Samaritans, which would make them Jews.

Lifelong enemies found themselves bound by what they understood to be a curse. When that curse was lifted, their bonds were broken, and it was back to being Samaritans and Jews. Only one knew that the healing went deeper than that; only one had the quality of faith that expresses itself in gratitude, the quality of faith that can make a person truly well.

94

Followers of Jesus say thank you to God.

Scope the

ZONE	TIME	SUPPLIES	⊚ ZONEZILLIES®
Zoom Into the Zone			
Get in the Zone	5 minutes	CD player	CD
Celebration Table	5 minutes	page 174, small table, white tablecloth, colored fabric, candle, Bible, thank-you card	none
Prepare a Litany	5 minutes	Reproducible 8B	click pen necklaces, spiked rubber ball
BibleZone®			
Enjoy the Story	5 minutes	Reproducible 8A	none
Thank You	5 minutes	Reproducible 8C, pencils	spiked rubber ball
Doodling Words	10 minutes	paper, markers	none
Affirmations	5 minutes	Reproducible 8D, CD player, safety pins	click pen necklaces, CD
LifeZone			
Praise 'n Prayer	10 minutes	Reproducibles 8B and 8E, Celebration Table, page 174, thank-you card, doodling pictures, CD player	CD

⊚ ZoneZillies® are found in the **BibleZone® LIVE FUNspirational® Kit.**

Zoom Into the Zone

Choose one or more activities to catch your children's interest.

Supplies:
CD player

ZoneZillies®:
CD

Get in the Zone

Play "Hallelujah Chorus" **(CD)** as the students arrive. Greet each student with a happy smile.

Say: Welcome to BibleZone Live! I'm glad you are here. This is the fun place where we will get to know the Bible as our book!

Supplies:
page 174
small table
white tablecloth
colored fabric
candle
Bible
thank-you card

ZoneZillies®:
none

Celebration Table

Ask one of the students who arrives early to help you prepare the Celebration Table. Cover the table and add a candle, a Bible, and colored fabric appropriate to the season, according to the instructions on page 12.

For this session place a thank-you card beside the candle.

Ask a student to prepare to read the closing prayer during your Praise 'n Prayer time. Give that student a copy of the prayer for week eight (page 174).

Supplies:
Reproducible 8B

ZoneZillies®:
click pen necklaces
spiked rubber ball

Prepare a Litany

Hand out **Reproducible 8B** and the **click pen necklaces**. Work together to fill in the litany.

Have each person fill in his or her copy with the words you select as a class. To do this, read the litany and then use the **spiked rubber ball** to ask for suggestions from the class for things that we thank God for. When a suggestion is given, encourage more thought by asking, "What is it about (*the suggestion*) that you are thankful for?" Encourage suggestions other than objects, such as a caring act that someone has done, opportunities to worship God, the privilege of worshiping without the government interfering, and so forth.

If you need additional space, use the back of the page. Ask the person who suggests a specific thanks to initial the space at the beginning of the line so that he or she knows to read it during the Praise 'n Prayer time.

Choose one or more activities to immerse your children in the Bible story.

Enjoy the Story

Hand out **Reproducible 8A** and read the story together.

Thank You

Hand out **Reproducible 8C** and read through the instructions with the students. After the students have connected each thank you and language, have them practice the languages. Have them each select one that they will use for the rest of the class.

Say: In our Bible story today the one person who returned to say thank you was a person from another region than the region Jesus was from—one where the people had been at odds with the Jews for centuries, and the Jews at odds with them. Though this man was considered a foreigner and a disliked one at that, he was appreciative enough to return and say thank you.

Ask: What are some other ways, rather than words, that we can say thank you to someone?

Use the **spiked rubber ball** to initiate discussion.

Answers:
Chinese: Xie Xie (shieh shieh)
French: merci (mehr SEE)
German: danke (DAHN kuh)
Greek: efharisto (eeyoo-khah-RISS-toh)
Russian: spasiba (spah-SEE-ba)
Spanish: gracias (GRAH-syahs)
Swahili: ahsante (uh-SAHN-the)
Arabic: sukran (soo-krahn)
Dutch: dank U (DAHNK-oo)
Portuguese: obrigado (oh-brih-GAH-doh)

Supplies:
Reproducible 8A

ZoneZillies®:
none

Supplies:
Reproducible 8C
pencils

ZoneZillies®:
spiked rubber ball

A Foreigner Shows the Way

(based on Luke 17:11-19)

by Delia Halverson

Jesus was walking along the road between Samaria and Galilee one day, heading for Jerusalem. As he approached a village, ten men stood at a distance and called to him.

It was not uncommon to see a band of people outside a village, usually in soiled and ragged clothing and living among the caves and rocks of the countryside. They often had to contend with the weather without even a tent for protection. When they saw someone approaching them, they were expected to call out, "Unclean! Unclean!" as a warning. You see, these people had a dreaded disease of the skin called leprosy. Leprosy was actually the name given to a whole assortment of skin diseases—anything from a simple rash to what is known as Hansen's Disease—that were characterized by large open sores, could cause fingers and toes to actually drop off, and were highly contagious.

Therefore, they were never allowed in the city or to come near anyone who did not have the disease.

These men stood away from Jesus and his friends, and instead of shouting "Unclean! Unclean!" they called out, "Jesus, Master, have pity on us!"

Jesus looked at them and said, "Go and show yourselves to the priests." The priests were the only people who could declare the lepers healed and give them permission to again be part of the community.

The men turned and went toward the village to find a priest. On their way they were healed of the leprosy.

When one of the men discovered that he had been healed, he turned around and went back to Jesus. He shouted praises to God and bowed down at Jesus' feet and thanked him.

This man was a foreigner, a Samaritan. It was unusual for Jews and Samaritans to be together, but he had been with the other nine. Jews considered Samaritans to be unclean, but when one is a leper, all other divisions become irrelevant. Yet this man was the only one to return and thank Jesus, and Jesus did notice. He said, "Weren't ten men healed? Where are the other nine? Why was the foreigner the only one who came back to thank God?"

Then Jesus told the man, "You may get up and go. Your faith has made you well."

98

Thanks Be to God

Leader: God, you have created us, and you desire that we worship you.

All: We worship you because we love you.

Leader: There are many things for which we give thanks.

Reader: We thank you for _____.

All: You are a great and loving God.

Reader: We thank you for _____.

All: You are a great and loving God.

Reader: We thank you for _____.

All: You are a great and loving God.

Reader: We thank you for _____.

All: You are a great and loving God.

Reader: We thank you for _____.

All: You are a great and loving God.

Reader: We thank you for _____.

All: You are a great and loving God.

Reader: We thank you for _____.

All: You are a great and loving God.

Reader: We thank you for _____.

All: You are a great and loving God.

Reader: We thank you for _____.

All: You are a great and loving God.

Leader: Like the one leper who returned to give Jesus thanks,

All: For all of these things, we thank you. Amen.

Thank You to All

Every language has its own words that mean thank you.
Match each language with its way of expressing thanks.

Chinese

French   *gracias*

danke

German

dank U   *obrigado*

Greek

Russian

efharisto   *merci*

Spanish

Swahili   *sukran*

ahsante

Arabic

                                    spasiba

Xie Xie

Dutch

Portuguese

Reproducible 8C

BibleZone® LIVE

Bible

Choose one or more activities to immerse your children in the Bible story.

Doodling Words

Supplies:
paper
markers

ZoneZillies®:
none

Give each student a piece of paper and markers and ask him or her to write "Thank You" in large script with a black marker, taking up most of the paper with the words.

Ask the students to use the markers to create a picture of things they thank God for, using colors to create the picture, but leaving the letters of the words in black so that it will stand out in the picture.

After the pictures are complete, have the students show their pictures to the class. Then ask them to place their doodling pictures on the Celebration Table until the end of the session.

Affirmations

Supplies:
Reproducible 8D
CD player
safety pins

ZoneZillies®:
click pen necklaces
CD

Hand out **Reproducible 8D** and the **click pen necklaces**. Ask each person to write his or her name at the top of the paper. Pin the papers on the backs of each person.

The students will move about the room, writing some positive thing about each person on the back of that person. Ask that they make sure that they write on each person's paper. It can be a characteristic of the person, or something as simple as liking the way a person smiles, or liking an item of clothing the person is wearing.

After the pages are complete, ask the students to remove their papers and find a place in the room where they are somewhat alone to read their own papers. Play "Jesu, Jesu" **(CD)** while they read their papers.

Life Zone

Choose one or more activities to bring the Bible to life.

Supplies:
Reproducibles 8B and 8E
Celebration Table
page 174
thank-you card
doodling pictures
CD player

ZoneZillies®:
CD

Praise 'n Prayer

Play "The Servant Song" **(CD)** to call the class to the Celebration Table for Praise 'n Prayer. Light the candle and call their attention to the appropriate seasonal color and the thank-you card on the table. Also call attention to the doodling pictures that they placed on the Celebration Table.

Ask: Why do we have the thank-you card and the doodling pictures you made on the Celebration Table?

After their comments, say a brief prayer: "We thank you, God, for all of these things, and we thank you for the opportunity to say thanks. Amen."

Read the litany you prepared using **Reproducible 8B**. Each person will read the line with the words he or she suggested, and the whole class will respond.

Hand out **Reproducible 8E**, "It Is Good to Give Thanks" **(CD)**. Listen to the song and then sing it together.

Ask the student you assigned earlier to close with the following prayer (also on page 174): "Our God, you are so great. Help us to be like the leper who remembered to return and thank Jesus for the healing. We want to always remember all that you do for us and your love for us. Amen."

Make a copy of HomeZone® for each student in your class.

Memory Verse
Your faith has made you well.

Luke 17:19

ThinkZone

God made the world and everything in it. God also made people. Why is it important to thank God for the things that people made?

Thank-You Pancakes

This recipe for pancakes with strawberry-orange sauce makes a good thank-you breakfast for a parent or anyone else whom you wish to thank.

Mix the sauce ahead of time and set aside: 1 package frozen, sliced strawberries (with sugar); 2 tablespoons frozen orange juice concentrate; and 1 tablespoon lemon juice.

Mash all together with a masher or fork and set aside. Use your favorite pancake recipe or try the following:

3 eggs
1 cup cottage cheese
½ cup flour
1 tablespoon sugar

1 tablespoon vegetable oil
1 teaspoon butter, melted
pinch of salt

Beat eggs and cottage cheese together with a fork, mixing well. Don't worry if the cottage cheese is a little lumpy. Add flour, sugar, melted butter and salt. Mix well. Heat a griddle or skillet with about a tablespoon vegetable oil. When the griddle is hot, pour out pancakes (about ½ cup batter for each pancake). When the pancakes bubble (about 2 minutes), turn them over and cook about a minute more until done.

Followers of Jesus say thank you to God.

Affirmations

_____,
(name)

you were made by God, and you were made special.
We thank God for the many ways you are special.

I thank God that _____.

I thank God that _____.

I thank God that _____.

I thank God that _____.

I thank God that _____.

I thank God that _____.

I thank God that _____.

I thank God that _____.

I thank God that _____.

I thank God that _____.

I thank God that _____.

I thank God that _____.

104

Reproducible 8D

BibleZone® LIVE

It Is Good to Give Thanks

It is good to give thanks.
It is good to give thanks to the Lord.
It is good to sing praises to the Lord's name.
It is good to give thanks to the Lord.

When we rise up in the morning,
we should all declare God's love.
Let us praise God every night
for watching from above.

It is good to give thanks.
It is good to give thanks to the Lord.
It is good to sing praises to the Lord's name.
It is good to give thanks to the Lord.

Let us praise God with our music;
raise your voices everyone.
Let us praise God for the wondrous things
that God has done.

It is good to give thanks.
It is good to give thanks to the Lord.
It is good to sing praises to the Lord's name.
It is good to give thanks to the Lord.

WORDS: Mark Burrows
MUSIC: Mark Burrows
© 2003 Abingdon Press, admin. by The Copyright Co., Nashville, TN 37212

Zacchaeus

Enter the Zone

Bible Verse
The Son of Man came to look for and to save people who are lost.

Luke 19:10

Bible Story
Luke 19:1-10

The Bible story of Zacchaeus encountering Jesus is one of the first that we tell our children. Young children, knowing what it is like to be small and unable to see over a crowd, enjoy the thought of climbing into a tree and looking down on a crowd. Revisiting this story as fourth, fifth, or sixth graders, your students will benefit from the ability to grasp a fuller understanding of the career of a tax collector in that era, and they will better understand a story that they might have previously seen as one primarily for younger children.

Jericho, situated in the valley of the Jordan River, was the river crossing for persons traveling east and west, and the primary approach to Jerusalem. Jews traveling from northern to southern Palestine on their way to Jerusalem often avoided Samaria by traveling on the east side of the Jordan and then crossing over to the west side of the Jordan. Jericho's famous balsam groves, date palms, and rose gardens made the city Palestine's richest tax center.

Rome determined the amount each district should be taxed and then farmed out the collection duties, selling the right to collect taxes to the highest bidder, who would in turn make a profit by charging the common people (who were unaware of the Roman rates) higher taxes. Some taxes—such as those paid for the privilege of being alive, the one-tenth paid on all grain grown and all wine or oil produced, and the income tax—were not very easy to change. But the duty taxes collected for use of the roads, markets, and harbors; on imports and exports; and on carts, cart wheels, and animals pulling the carts gave collectors ample opportunity to grow wealthy. Tax collectors could even stop persons on the road and make them unpack their bundles, charging tax on the contents. If unable to pay the taxes, persons were sometimes loaned the money at a high rate of interest by the tax collector.

So it was that the diminutive and hated Zacchaeus found himself in need of the healing acceptance he received from Jesus.

Followers of Jesus love and accept others.

Scope the

ZONE	TIME	SUPPLIES	⊙ ZONEZILLIES®
Zoom Into the Zone			
Get in the Zone	5 minutes	CD player	CD
Celebration Table	5 minutes	page 174, small table, white tablecloth, colored fabric, candle, Bible, closed box with a mirror inside on the bottom	none
BibleZone®			
God Loves All	5 minutes	Reproducible 9C, Bibles	spiked rubber ball, click pen necklaces
Enjoy the Story	5 minutes	Reproducibles 9A–9B, Bible	none
Cookies for Sharing God's Love	10 minutes	tube icing with decorating tips; flat, plain cookies (at least four per student—three for sharing and one for eating)	none
Each Unique	10 minutes	box with mirror	spiked rubber ball
LifeZone			
Dial-a-Verse	5 minutes	Bibles, Reproducible 9D, pencils	none
Praise 'n Prayer	10 minutes	Reproducible 9E, Celebration Table, page 174, mirror, CD player	CD

⊙ ZoneZillies® are found in the **BibleZone® LIVE FUNspirational® Kit.**

Zoom Into the Zone

Choose one or more activities to catch your children's interest.

Supplies:
CD player

ZoneZillies®:
CD

Supplies:
page 174
small table
white tablecloth
colored fabric
candle
Bible
closed box with a
    mirror inside on the
    bottom

ZoneZillies®:
none

Get in the Zone

Play "Hallelujah Chorus" **(CD)** as the students arrive. Greet each student with a happy smile.

Say: Welcome to BibleZone Live! I'm glad you are here. This is the fun place where we will get to know the Bible as our book!

Celebration Table

Ask one of the students who arrives early to help you prepare the Celebration Table.

Cover the table and add a candle, a Bible, and colored fabric appropriate to the season, according to the instructions on page 12.

For this session have a mirror in the bottom of a box with a lid. Place the closed box with the mirror beside the candle.

Ask a student to prepare to read the closing prayer during your Praise 'n Prayer time. Give that student a copy of the prayer for week nine (page 174).

Choose one or more activities to immerse your children in the Bible story.

God Loves All

Hand out **Reproducible 9C** and have the students read the section at the top. Hand out Bibles and the **click pen necklaces**. Divide the class into seven groups and assign each group one of the references to look up in the Bible. Ask them to review the passage. Select someone to read it to the class. With the reading of each passage, use the **spiked rubber ball** and ask the students what they know about that person.

Below are some things that you might bring out. Encourage the students to make notes about the persons on their papers.

Genesis 1:27—Adam and Eve (We are made in God's image.)
Genesis 17:15-19—Abraham and Sarah (God accepts us even when we are not perfect; God keeps promises.)
Exodus 2:1-3; 3:1-4, 10—Moses (God calls us for special acts.)
1 Samuel 16:1, 7-13—David (God sees us on the inside more than the outside.)
Jeremiah 1:4-9—Jeremiah (God calls us even when we are young.)
Mark 1:9-11—Jesus (God sent a special person to tell us how to live peacefully with God and with one another.)
Matthew 4:18-22; Mark 2:13-15—Disciples (Jesus chose ordinary persons as his disciples, some whose capabilities others might have doubted.)

Say: God made each of us unique and calls each of us to follow Jesus in our own unique way. The people we've mentioned had specific tasks to do for God. In the next sessions of our quarter, we will learn about other people who took on their special tasks and carried on God's message after Jesus died. Today our story is about someone whom most people hated, but whom Jesus accepted.

Enjoy the Story

Read Luke 19:1-10 from the Bible. Hand out **Reproducibles 9A–9B**. Divide the class into two sides and read the story litany together.

Supplies:
Reproducible 9C
Bibles

ZoneZillies®:
spiked rubber ball
click pen necklaces

Supplies:
Reproducibles 9A–9B
Bible

ZoneZillies®:
none

A Lesson of Love

(based on Luke 19:1–10)

by James H. Ritchie Jr.

Side A: A man named Zacchaeus,

Side B: (so short he can't see us),

Side A: in Jericho dwelt—

Side B: and his tale makes us melt!

Side A: This short tax collector,

Side B: (a good will rejecter),

Side A: was placed on Rome's payroll

Side B: to gather the road toll.

Side A: His own thought him mere scum

Side B: for taxing their income,

Side A: their travel, their trading;

Side B: so thoughtlessly raiding

Side A: their pockets, expecting

Side B: great wealth from collecting.

Side A: Quite rich did old Zach grow,

Side B: since nothing he lacked, so

Side A: he figured he'd made it.

Side B: The truth? He was hated!

Side A: Then, Jericho-bound,

Side B: Jesus came, looked around.

Side A: In a sycamore tree

Side B: taxing Zach did he see.

Side A: Spite a city-wide frown,

Side B: Jesus said, "Zach, come down!

Side A: They'll grump and they'll grouse,

Side B: but I'm aimed for your house

Side A: with some needed advice—

Side B: and a meal would be nice."

Side A: Zacchaeus descended.

Side B: The crowd, quite offended,

Side A: called, "Why should this sinner

Side B: take Jesus to dinner?"

Side A: It was right, it was good.

Side B: After dinner, Zach stood,

Side A: looked at Jesus, still seated,

Side B: Confessed, "I have cheated.

110

Reproducible 9A

Side A: I'll give half my stuff

Side B: to the poor. Not enough?

Side A: Four times what I stole,

Side B: I'll pay back. Save my soul!"

Side A: "Now this," Jesus claimed,

Side B: "is right where I have aimed.

Side A: Regardless of cost,

Side B: I've come seeking the lost.

Side A: Though you rudely behaved,

Side B: you and your brood are saved!

Side A: Now true to your past,

Side B: you've been faithful at last!

Side A: If ever t'was one,

Side B: this is Abraham's son!"

God Loves All

God has made each of us special and unique.
There have been many people in the past who have helped us understand God.
God used these people to bring about a more loving and peaceful world.
Here are a few that you can read about in your Bibles. Look up the references
in the Bible and write what we can learn from these people.

Genesis 1:27

_____

_____

Genesis 17:15-19

_____

_____

Exodus 2:1-3; 3:1-4, 10

_____

_____

1 Samuel 16:1, 7-13

_____

_____

Jeremiah 1:4-9

_____

_____

Mark 1:9-11

_____

_____

Matthew 4:18-22; Mark 2:13-15

_____

Reproducible 9C

BIBLEZONE® LIV

Choose one or more activities to immerse your children in the Bible story.

Cookies for Sharing God's Love

Say: Jesus shared a meal with someone who was not loved by many people. We are going to share some cookies among ourselves. We will also write messages on cookies that we can share with others. You may want to write "God loves you" or "Made by God." When you share the cookies, you can tell the people who receive them that God loves them and made them special. After class, take the cookies home to share with a friend or relative. Or you may know someone here at church you would like to tell about God's love and with whom you'd like to share a cookie.

NOTE: If you have plenty of time, you can bake your own cookies, using a plain sugar cookie recipe.

Supplies:
tube icing with decorating tips
flat plain cookies (at least four per student—three for sharing and one for eating)

ZoneZillies®:
none

Each Unique

Arrange chairs in a circle, but keep them slightly apart from one another. After the students are seated, take the closed box from the Celebration Table and hold it in your lap. Use the **spiked rubber ball** to guide conversation and give everyone a chance to speak.

Say: Can you think of an object in this church that is unique because there is only one like it? How about in the community where we live? How about in our state? How about in our world? (*Allow for responses to each question.*) What you will find in this box is unique. There's not another like it in the world because God made only one. I'm going to stand in front of each of you and allow you to peek inside to see what is there, but you mustn't tell anyone else what you see.

Move from student to student, opening the box so that only one person at a time can see the mirror inside and his or her reflection. After all have looked, continue the conversation.

Ask: Was I correct? Is there another just like the one in the box? (*Allow for responses.*) We were each made special by God. Last week we talked about and thanked God for that specialness. Our story today told about a man whom Jesus found worthy of acceptance, even when others rejected him.

Supplies:
box with mirror

ZoneZillies®:
spiked rubber ball

Choose one or more activities to bring the Bible to life.

Supplies:
Bibles
Reproducible 9D
pencils

ZoneZillies®:
none

Supplies:
Reproducible 9E
Celebration Table
page 174
mirror
CD player

ZoneZillies®:
CD

Dial-a-Verse

Hand out Bibles, **Reproducible 9D**, and pencils.

Make sure that the students understand the directions.

Praise 'n Prayer

Play "The Servant Song" **(CD)** to call the class to the Celebration Table for Praise 'n Prayer.

Light the candle and call their attention to the appropriate seasonal color and the mirror on the table.

Ask: Why do you suppose we have the mirror on the Celebration Table? (*to remind us that we are each made unique and special by God*)

Hand out **Reproducible 9E** ("One of a Kind"). Sing the song together **(CD)**.

Ask the student you assigned earlier to close with the following prayer (also on page 174): "Our God, some think that being different means being better than others, and some think it means being worse. Help us to remember that you think we are all special, and remind us that we are called and prepared to do special things for you. Amen."

Make a copy of HomeZone® for each student in your class.

114

LOVING REMINDER

Make a small scarf or hanging as a reminder that God created each of us different and yet loves us all. You'll need a ten-inch square of sandpaper and wax crayons. Draw faces of people on the sandpaper and write "God Loves Us All" on the sandpaper. Place a twelve-inch square of white fabric over the sandpaper and iron it with a moderately hot iron. (Protect the working surface from the heat of the iron.) The design will transfer onto the fabric with an interesting, textured look.

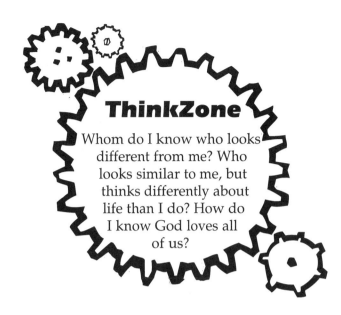

ThinkZone

Whom do I know who looks different from me? Who looks similar to me, but thinks differently about life than I do? How do I know God loves all of us?

Memory Verse

The Son of Man came to look for and to save people who are lost.

Luke 19:10

Different Muffins

You will need: 2 cups all-purpose flour; 2 teaspoons baking powder; ½ teaspoon salt; ½ cup softened butter; 1 cup sugar; 2 eggs; ⅓ cup milk; sugar; and assorted fruits and nuts (strawberry, blueberry, small pieces of apple, raisins, and so forth).

Combine the dry ingredients and set them aside. In a large bowl, beat butter and sugar at a medium speed until well blended. Add eggs and beat until smooth. Add several spoons of the flour mixture and milk, alternating until it is all mixed together. Spoon into a paper-lined, 12-cup muffin tin. Place pieces of fruit or nuts in each muffin, using a different one for each cup. Push the fruit or nuts down into the batter. Sprinkle sugar over the top of each muffin and bake in a 450-degree preheated oven for 5 minutes. Reduce the heat to 375 degrees and bake 30–35 more minutes or until the muffins spring back when lightly touched with your finger.

Followers of Jesus love and accept others.

Dial – a – Cell Verse

Use the cell phone code below to read the Bible verse for today. Look at the sets of numbers below. The first number in each set will tell you which button on the cell phone to find. The second number will tell you which letter on that button to choose. Write that letter on the line above the set of numbers. For example, 4-2 means to look at button 4 and then choose the second letter. The letter you will choose will be H. After you have written it from the code, turn to the verse in the Bible and check your work. Your Bible's translation may be a little different from the one used in the code.

T H E   S O N   O F
8-1 4-2 3-2   7-4 6-3 6-2   6-3 3-3

M A N   C A M E
6-1 2-1 6-2   2-3 2-1 6-1 3-2

T O   L O O K   F O R
8-1 6-3   5-3 6-3 6-3 5-2   3-3 6-3 7-3

A N D   T O   S A V E
2-1 6-2 3-1   8-1 6-3   7-4 2-1 8-3 3-2

P E O P L E   W H O
7-1 3-2 6-3 7-1 5-3 3-2   9-1 4-2 6-3

A R E   L O S T.
2-1 7-3 3-2   5-3 6-3 7-4 8-1

Luke 19:10

116

Reproducible 9D

BIBLEZONE® LIVE

One of a Kind

No one in this whole wide world was made the same as you.
No one else can walk your walk or do the things you do.
So hold your head up high. You're the apple of God's eye.
You're the only you like you. You're one of a kind.

No one in the whole wide world was made the same as me.
No one else can laugh my laugh or be what I can be.
I'll hold my head up high. I'm the apple of God's eye.
I'm the only me like me. I'm one of a kind.

In God's eyes there's no second class, no wimp, no slob, no geek.
So let your light shine for the world. You're special, you're unique.

Each of us has special gifts that only we can bring.
Each of us has our own style and our own song to sing.
No matter big or small, God made and loves us all.
I'm the only me like me. I'm one of a kind.
He's the only he like he. She's the only she like she.
I'm the only me like me. I'm one of a kind.

WORDS: Mark Burrows
MUSIC: Mark Burrows
Copyright © 2004 by Abingdon Press

Blind Bartimaeus

Enter the

Bible Verse
Your heavenly Father is even more ready to give good things to people who ask.
Matthew 7:11

Bible Story
Mark 10:46-52

In spite of the absence of today's communications technology, news of Jesus' presence in Jericho must have traveled fast, resulting in the crowd that followed him. Although religious law required every male Hebrew within a fifteen-mile radius of Jerusalem to observe the Passover there, this travel was impossible for many. Plan B was to wait along the main street of Jericho (which was also the road to Jerusalem), watch for learned rabbis or teachers passing through on their way to the Passover celebration, and walk along with them as they taught and traveled through town.

Bartimaeus, attempting to take advantage of the generosity of the Passover pilgrims, was begging at the northern gate of the city when he heard the crowd approaching and caught wind that it was the miracle-working rabbi named Jesus around whom the crowd had assembled. Believing that Jesus could cure his blindness, Bartimaeus determined that it would take a major disturbance in order to attract Jesus' attention. When Bartimaeus

called out to Jesus and Jesus answered him, Bartimaeus knew it was the chance of a lifetime, and he took it. He was ready to respond to the call of Jesus.

How often do we sense Jesus' call, but, fearing that we will be ridiculed by others or that it will take too much time, opt not to answer? We want an intimate relationship with God, but not a demanding one.

In calling upon Jesus as the Son of David, Bartimaeus understood him to be a messiah who would unite the world by force, as did David. Jesus healed Bartimaeus even though he still had miles to go on his theological journey after his sight was restored. We cannot expect persons to have all the answers when they first encounter Christ. Understanding comes only with continued reflection upon one's own life and wrestling with questions of faith. Teachers have the opportunity to nurture that development.

Followers of Jesus ask for help.

Scope the Zone

ZONE	TIME	SUPPLIES	⊚ ZONEZILLIES®
Zoom Into the Zone			
Get in the Zone	5 minutes	CD player	CD
Celebration Table	5 minutes	page 174, small table, white tablecloth, colored fabric, candle, Bible, sign with a large question mark	none
God Helps	5 minutes	Reproducible 10C, pencils	none
BibleZone®			
Turn to the Bible	5 minutes	Bibles, Reproducible 10D, pencils	none
Enjoy the Story	10 minutes	Reproducibles 10A–10B (optional: rhythm instruments)	none
Ask Jesus for Help	10 minutes	crayons, iron, sandpaper (6 by 7 inches or smaller) for each student, light-colored construction paper	none
How Far to Go?	10 minutes	blindfolds, pencils, paper	striped beach balls, tape measure key chains
LifeZone			
Praise 'n Prayer	10 minutes	Celebration Table, page 174, question mark sign, Reproducible 10E, CD player, sandpaper pictures	spiked rubber ball, CD

⊚ ZoneZillies® are found in the **BibleZone® LIVE FUNspirational® Kit.**

Zoom Into the Zone

Choose one or more activities to catch your children's interest.

Supplies:
CD player

ZoneZillies®:
CD

Get in the Zone

Play "Hallelujah Chorus" **(CD)** as the students arrive. Greet each student with a happy smile.

Say: Welcome to BibleZone Live! I'm glad you are here. This is the fun place where we will get to know the Bible as our book!

Supplies:
page 174
small table
white tablecloth
colored fabric
candle
Bible
sign with a large
    question mark

ZoneZillies®:
none

Celebration Table

Ask one of the students who arrives early to help you prepare the Celebration Table.

Cover the table and add a candle, a Bible, and colored fabric appropriate to the season, according to the instructions on page 12.

For this session place a sign with a large question mark beside the candle.

Ask a student to prepare to read the closing prayer during your Praise 'n Prayer time. Give that student a copy of the prayer for week ten (page 174).

Supplies:
Reproducible 10C
pencils

ZoneZillies®:
none

God Helps

Hand out **Reproducible 10C** and pencils. Be sure that the students understand the instructions.

120

Bible

Choose one or more activities to immerse your children in the Bible story.

Turn to the Bible

Hand out Bibles and ask the students to turn to Mark 10:46-52. Ask someone to read the story from the Bible.

Then hand out **Reproducible 10D** and pencils and read the information at the top. Be sure that the students understand the instructions.

Enjoy the Story

Hand out **Reproducibles 10A–10B**, "Go, Bartimaeus: Rap Version." Determine right and left sides and assign parts for Narrator, Bartimaeus, Solo, and Jesus.

Create the rap accompaniment with body percussion—leg pats or finger snaps, or with rhythm instruments that are available. During the verses (everything but the beginning and the refrains), those who aren't speaking can say very softly along with the body percussion, "Go! Go! Go! Go!"

Read the rap through at least a couple of times.

Supplies:
Bibles
Reproducible 10D
pencils

ZoneZillies®:
none

Supplies:
Reproducibles
   10A–10B
optional: rhythm
   instruments

ZoneZillies®:
none

Go, Bartimaeus: Rap Version

(based on Mark 10:46-52)

by James H. Ritchie, Jr.

REFRAIN:
Right: Go!
Left: Go!
Right: Go!
Left: Go!
Right: Bartimaeus, go!
Left: Go!
All: Go, Bartimaeus; your faith has made you well!
Right: Go!
Left: Go!
Right: Go!
Left: Bartimaeus, go!
Right: Go!
All: Go, Bartimaeus; your faith has made you well!
Left: Go, go, go, go!
Right: Go, go, go!

Narrator: Jesus and his followers were leaving Jericho.
From the street they heard a voice as they prepared to go.
Over all the city noise, as clear as it could be:

Bartimaeus: Jesus, Son of David, have mercy on me!

REFRAIN:
Right: Go!
Left: Go!
Right: Go!
Left: Go!
Right: Bartimaeus, go!
Left: Go!
All: Go, Bartimaeus; your faith has made you well!
Right: Go!

Left: Go!
Right: Go!
Left: Bartimaeus, go!
Right: Go!
All: Go, Bartimaeus; your faith has made you well!
Left: Go, go, go, go!
Right: Go, go, go!

Narrator: News had traveled through the crowd and Bartimaeus heard.
Though the beggar couldn't see he seldom missed a word.
Sensing Jesus near at hand, he shouted forcefully:

Bartimaeus: Jesus, Son of David, have mercy on me!

REFRAIN:
Right: Go!
Left: Go!
Right: Go!
Left: Go!
Right: Bartimaeus, go!
Left: Go!
All: Go, Bartimaeus; your faith has made you well!
Right: Go!
Left: Go!
Right: Go!
Left: Bartimaeus, go!
Right: Go!
All: Go, Bartimaeus; your faith has made you well!
Left: Go, go, go, go!
Right: Go, go, go!

Reproducible 10A

BibleZone® Live

Narrator: Some cried out,

Solo: Be quiet! Oh the trouble you could cause!

Narrator: But the shouting prompted Jesus and his friends to pause. Jesus said,

Jesus: Go call the one who cries unceasingly:

Bartimaeus: Jesus, Son of David, have mercy on me!

REFRAIN:
Right: Go!
Left: Go!
Right: Go!
Left: Go!
Right: Bartimaeus, go!
Left: Go!
All: Go, Bartimaeus; your faith has made you well!
Right: Go!
Left: Go!
Right: Go!
Left: Bartimaeus, go!
Right: Go!
All: Go, Bartimaeus; your faith has made you well!
Left: Go, go, go, go!
Right: Go, go, go!

Solo: Take heart, Bartimaeus, Jesus wants to speak with you.

Narrator: Throwing off his coat he jumped and through the crowd he flew.
Jesus welcomes he who cried enthusiastically:

Bartimaeus: Jesus, Son of David, have mercy on me!

REFRAIN:
Right: Go!
Left: Go!
Right: Go!
Left: Go!
Right: Bartimaeus, go!
Left: Go!

All: Go, Bartimaeus; your faith has made you well!
Right: Go!
Left: Go!
Right: Go!
Left: Bartimaeus, go!
Right: Go!
All: Go, Bartimaeus; your faith has made you well!
Left: Go, go, go, go!
Right: Go, go, go!

Jesus: What is it,

Narrator: asked Jesus,

Jesus: that you want for me to do?

Bartimaeus: Teacher, let me see again. That's what I ask of you.

Narrator: Sight returned to he who dared to shout out faithfully:

Bartimaeus: Jesus, Son of David, have mercy on me!

REFRAIN:
Right: Go!
Left: Go!
Right: Go!
Left: Go!
Right: Bartimaeus, go!
Left: Go!
All: Go, Bartimaeus; your faith has made you well!
Right: Go!
Left: Go!
Right: Go!
Left: Bartimaeus, go!
Right: Go!
All: Go, Bartimaeus; your faith has made you well!
Left: Go, go, go, go!
Right: Go, go, go!

WORDS: James Ritchie (based on Mark 10:46-52)
MUSIC: James Ritchie
© 1991 by James Ritchie. Used by permission.
Rap arrangement by James Ritchie. © 2005 by James Ritchie.
Used by permission.

God Helps, Others Help, and I Help

Bartimaeus believed that Jesus could help him, but he first made a disturbance to get Jesus' attention. He helped himself, and disciples helped by urging him to come to Jesus. God can help us through many hard times. Sometimes the way that God helps is through other people. Sometimes God helps us by urging us to help ourselves. Fill in the following blanks to complete the sentences.

	God Helps	Others Help	I Help
When I have a test			
When my friend snubs me			
When I disagree with a parent			
When I am sick			
When I am afraid			
When I have a difficult task			

124

Reproducible 10C

BIBLEZONE® LIVE

Choose one or more activities to immerse your children in the Bible story.

Ask Jesus for Help

Hand out crayons, a piece of fine-grade sandpaper (if possible, an aluminum oxide sandpaper without resin) for each student, and a sheet of light-colored construction paper. Have the students draw a large, fat question mark in the center of their sandpaper, using plenty of crayon. Also have them write the ZoneIn phrase, "Followers of Jesus ask for help," and add any other decorations they like.

Read the ZoneIn phrase together, then have each student transfer the question mark and design from the sandpaper to the construction paper by placing the sandpaper face up on an ironing surface, with the construction paper on top and completely covering the crayon. With an iron set on low, iron the paper until the crayon wax begins to bleed through the construction paper. After it is ironed, remove the paper and save it and the sandpaper for the Praise 'n Prayer time.

Supplies:
crayons
iron
sandpaper (6 by 7
    inches or smaller)
    for each student
light-colored
    construction paper

ZoneZillies®:
none

How Far to Go?

Say: Bartimaeus had faith in Jesus' healing power, but he didn't understand that Jesus was a messiah who came in peace. We know that because Bartimaeus called out "Son of David," which referred to a messiah who would come as a military hero, as did David, and who would overthrow the Roman government, restoring the land to the Jews. Although Bartimaeus had a strong faith, he had a long way to go in his theological understanding about Jesus.

Divide the class into two or three teams, depending on the size of the class.

Say: We are going to play a game where each one of you will be blindfolded, and you will try to throw a ball as far as you can. Before each person throws the ball, the team will shout, "Go, Bartimaeus, how long 'til you know?" Someone from your team will be appointed as the measurer. After each throw, the measurer will use a tape measure key chain **to record the distance of the throw. The total distances of all of the throws will be added together to see how far Bartimaeus has to go in his faith journey for your team.**

If the teams are small, let each player throw two times.

Supplies:
blindfolds
pencils
paper

ZoneZillies®:
striped beach balls
tape measure key
    chains

Choose one or more activities to bring the Bible to life.

Supplies:
Celebration Table
page 174
question mark sign
Reproducible 10E
CD player
sandpaper pictures

ZoneZillies®:
spiked rubber ball
CD

Praise 'n Prayer

Play "The Servant Song" **(CD)** to call the class to the Celebration Table for Praise 'n Prayer. Light the candle and call their attention to the appropriate seasonal color and the question mark on the table.

Ask the students to hold their paper with the question mark and sandpaper. Use the **spiked rubber ball** to facilitate conversation about the following:

Say: Feel the reproducible and feel the sandpaper. How are they different? When have you felt that you had a rough time and needed Jesus' help? When has a situation been smoother after you had help? How does the question mark on our Celebration Table remind you of our story today? Who asked Jesus for help in our story?

Read the ZoneIn phrase together.

Hand out **Reproducible 10E**, "Go, Bartimaeus."

Say: The words to this song are similar to the words from the rap that we've already performed. Pay attention once again to the words and the story of Bartimaeus.

Assign parts for Jesus, the Disciple, Bartimaeus, and the Character voices. Everyone else will be in the Chorus. Play through a verse to give them an idea of the tune of "Go, Bartimaeus" **(CD)**, and then encourage them to sing along with the CD.

Ask the student you assigned earlier to close with the following prayer (also on page 174): "Our God, we thank you that we can ask you for help. We know that you will help us even in hard times and that sometimes you send others to help us. Amen."

Make a copy of HomeZone® for each student in your class.

BREATH PRAYER

Write a breath prayer that will help you through tough times. A breath prayer is a prayer that can be said in one breath. It can be said at any time and at any place. Here are some suggestions for writing it.

Find a quiet place and close your eyes, remembering that God loves you. Imagine God calling you by name and asking what you need in order to be whole or well. Answer God with one or two words or a short phrase, such as *courage*, *peace*, or *forgiveness*. Choose your favorite name for God: *God, Jesus, Christ, Lord, Spirit, Creator*. Combine your name for God with your answer to God's question. It may be: "Give me courage, O God." Or "Jesus, I need to not worry so much." Change the words around so that they flow smoothly as you breathe. Say or think the words of the prayer as you breathe in and breathe out. Write the prayer down and use it several times during the day. It will become part of your life.

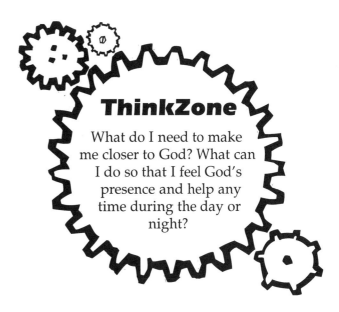

ThinkZone

What do I need to make me closer to God? What can I do so that I feel God's presence and help any time during the day or night?

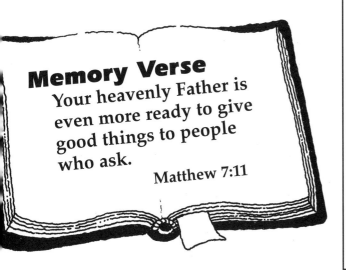

Memory Verse

Your heavenly Father is even more ready to give good things to people who ask.

Matthew 7:11

Peanut Butter French Toast

6 slices bread
½ cup preserves or jelly, any flavor
½ cup creamy peanut butter
½ cup eggs, beaten well
½ cup milk
2 tablespoons butter

Spread preserves evenly over three slices of bread. Spread peanut better evenly over remaining three slices of bread. Press preserves and peanut butter slices together to form three sandwiches; cut each diagonally in half. Combine egg and milk in a shallow bowl.

Heat a grill or skillet with butter. Dip each sandwich in the egg mixture to coat, and cook in butter on the grill or skillet about two minutes per side or until golden. Keep warm and serve with syrup or honey. Makes six servings.

Followers of Jesus ask for help.

By the Side of the Road

The words hidden in this picture make up the Bible verse found in Matthew 7:11.
Find the words and circle them. Then turn to the verse in the Bible and use the
words you found to write the verse on the lines below. Remember that your
Bible's translation may be different from the translation with these words, so
you must find the ones in the picture to have the right words.

Matthew 7:11

Followers of Jesus ask for help.

Reproducible 10D

BibleZone® LIVE

Go, Bartimaeus

Refrain:
Go, go, Bartimaeus, go!
Go, Bartimaeus; your faith has made you well!
Go, Bartimaeus, go!
Go, Bartimaeus; your faith has made you well!

(*Chorus*) Jesus and his followers were leaving Jericho.
From the street they heard a voice as they prepared to go.
Over all the city noise, as clear as it could be:
(*Bartimaeus*) "Jesus, son of David, have mercy on me!"

REFRAIN

(*Chorus*) News had traveled through the crowd and Bartimaeus heard.
Though the beggar couldn't see he seldom missed a word.
Sensing Jesus near at hand, he shouted forcefully:
(*Bartimaeus*) "Jesus, son of David, have mercy on me!"

REFRAIN

(*Voices*) Some cried out, "Be quiet! Oh, the trouble you could cause!"
(*Chorus*) But the shouting prompted Jesus and his friends to pause.
(*Jesus*) Jesus said, "Go call the one who shouts unceasingly:
(*Bartimaeus*) "Jesus, son of David, have mercy on me!"

REFRAIN

(*Disciple*) "Take heart, Bartimaeus, Jesus wants to speak with you."
(*Chorus*) Throwing off his coat he jumped and through the crowd he flew.
Jesus welcomed he who cried enthusiastically:
(*Bartimaeus*) "Jesus, son of David, have mercy on me!"

REFRAIN

(*Jesus*) "What is it," asked Jesus, "that you want for me to do?"
(*Bartimaeus*) "Teacher, let me see again. That's what I ask of you!"
Sight returned to he who dared to shout out faithfully:
(*Bartimaeus*) "Jesus, son of David, have mercy on me!"

REFRAIN

WORDS: James Ritchie (based on Mark 10:46-52)
MUSIC: James Ritchie
ARRANGEMENT: Linda Ray Miller
Words and music copyright © 1991 by James Ritchie. Arrangement copyright © 1995 by Cokesbury.

The Damascus Road

Enter the

Bible Verse

[God] chose me to be a servant of Christ Jesus.

Romans 15:16, adapted

Bible Story

Acts 9:1-19

An amazing turnabout positioned a passionate Pharisee named Saul to become a great missionary of Christ. Present at the stoning of Stephen, Saul could hardly have avoided the impact of the early Christian martyr's words and actions. Later, on his way to arrest Damascus Christians whom he believed to threaten the faith about which he was so passionate, Saul was blinded by a light—perhaps a delayed awareness of Stephen's message.

All new Christians need mentors to help them grow in faith, so God sent Ananias to heal Saul's sight and lead him in the path of his calling. Known later by his Greek name, Paul, he became mentor to many churches that sprang up in the world around the Mediterranean Sea, focusing his efforts on reaching the Greek-speaking world. As we follow the life of Paul during the years between the Damascus Road experience and his active missionary ministry, we realize that Paul spent many years in preparation

for his new ministry (see Galatians 1:13—2:1). Though his turnabout seemed sudden and his mission work an immediate product of his conversion, Saul was being prepared by God for both his conversion and his mission.

Ananias, Saul's remarkable mentor, took a great risk in answering God's call to tell a persecutor of Christians about Jesus. It could have been a trap leading to his arrest. But Ananias set a great example of Christian forgiveness and hospitality, addressing his adversary as "brother." In this atmosphere of forgiveness, Saul's sight was restored, and the course was set for the missionary work that transformed the church.

Whether our decision to follow Christ comes suddenly or after years of experience in the church or with Christian people, we need to be ready to follow when God calls us—prepared to use our gifts, graces, and experiences in effective discipleship for Jesus Christ and his church.

Jesus calls us to be disciples.

Scope the

ZONE	TIME	SUPPLIES	⊚ ZONEZILLIES®
Zoom Into the Zone			
Get in the Zone	5 minutes	CD player	CD
Celebration Table	5 minutes	page 174, small table, white tablecloth, colored fabric, candle, Bible, pair of running shoes	none
Running Crossword Puzzle	5 minutes	Reproducible 11C	click pen necklaces
BibleZone®			
Turn to the Bible	5 minutes	Bibles	none
Enjoy the Story	10 minutes	Reproducibles 11A–11B (optional: biblical costume)	spiked rubber ball
Reminder Crosses	10 minutes	Reproducible 11D, masking tape, plastic wrap, watercolor or tempera paint, trays or shallow dishes, newspaper or other table protection, cleanup supplies	click pen necklaces
Are You the Disciple?	10 minutes	small pieces of paper, basket	click pen necklaces
LifeZone			
Praise 'n Prayer	10 minutes	page 174, Celebration Table, running shoes, Reproducible 11E, CD player	CD

⊚ ZoneZillies® are found in the **BibleZone® LIVE FUNspirational® Kit.**

Zoom Into the ⊚ZONE

Choose one or more activities to catch your children's interest.

Supplies:
CD player

ZoneZillies®:
CD

Get in the Zone

Play "Hallelujah Chorus" (**CD**) as the students arrive. Greet each student with a happy smile.

Say: Welcome to BibleZone Live! I'm glad you are here. This is the fun place where we will get to know the Bible as our book!

Supplies:
page 174
small table
white tablecloth
colored fabric
candle
Bible
pair of running shoes

ZoneZillies®:
none

Celebration Table

Ask one of the students who arrives early to help you prepare the Celebration Table. Cover the table and add a candle, a Bible, and colored fabric appropriate to the season, according to the instructions on page 12. For this session place running shoes beside the candle.

Ask a student to prepare to read the closing prayer during your Praise 'n Prayer time. Give that student a copy of the prayer for week eleven (page 174).

Supplies:
Reproducible 11C

ZoneZillies®:
click pen necklaces

Running Crossword Puzzle

Hand out **Reproducible 11C** and **click pen necklaces**. Be sure that the students understand that the words in the puzzle have to do with running.

Crossword puzzle answers:
1. race
2. start
3. finish
4. relay
5. track
6. sprint
7. teams
8. trophy
9. Christ

132

Bible

Choose one or more activities to immerse your children in the Bible story.

Turn to the Bible

Hand out Bibles and ask the students to turn to Romans 15:16. Read the Bible verse together.

Say: Our story today is about Paul, who once said, "I have finished the race, and I have been faithful." Remember, you read about this on your crossword puzzle page.

Supplies:
Bibles

ZoneZillies®:
none

Enjoy the Story

Hand out **Reproducibles 11A–11B** and either read the story or tell it as if you were Ananias. You may want to dress in biblical costume or have someone come in dressed as Ananias to tell the story.

After the story, use the **spiked rubber ball** to initiate discussion.

Ask: Were you already familiar with the story of Ananias? Describe how you might have responded had you been directed by God to bring healing to the "enemy." How did Saul (also known by his Greek name, Paul) respond to Christ's call? Whom do you know who has said yes to Christ's call? How many ways can you name by which Christ calls persons into ministry?

Supplies:
Reproducibles
   11A–11B
optional: biblical
   costume

ZoneZillies®:
spiked rubber ball

Ananias' Story

(based on Acts 9:1-19)

by Delia Halverson

My name is Ananias (an-uh-NIE-uhs), and my story, unbelievable as it sounds, is absolutely true.

My home was the beautiful city of Damascus, the capital of Syria. Because of the many rivers and streams flowing through the area, Damascus is like one huge garden. It is also the intersection of three caravan routes, making it a cultural center and a hub for sending messages all over the world—at least that part of the world we know.

When this story took place, among the Jews in Damascus there were a number of people who believed that Jesus, crucified and risen, was the Messiah. I was one of them. Actually, the story began on the road to Damascus, where a very intense traveler unexpectedly found himself knocked to the ground by an even more intense light.

Without knowing what was happening on the road outside Damascus, Jesus spoke to me very plainly in my prayers—as plainly as I am speaking to you. "Get up," he said, "and go to the house of Judas on Straight Street." This was another Judas, by the way, not Judas Iscariot the disciple, who had betrayed Jesus. Jesus went on to say, "When you get there, you will find a man named Saul from the city of Tarsus. Saul is praying, and he has seen a vision. He saw

a man named Ananias coming to him and putting his hands on him, so that he could see again."

I had heard stories about this man, Saul, and wasn't feeling particularly overjoyed at Jesus' words. To be honest, they frightened and even angered me! Saul, blind? He deserved it! I replied, "Lord, a lot of people have told me about the terrible things this man has done to your followers in Jerusalem. Now the chief priests have given him the power to come here and arrest anyone who worships in your name." It sounded to me like someone I needed to avoid like the plague!

Jesus understood my dilemma, I'm sure, but that didn't change anything. "Go!" he said. "I have chosen Saul to tell foreigners, kings, and the people of Israel about me. I will show him how much he must suffer for worshiping in my name."

I'll admit, the thought of Saul suffering did have its appeal, considering the suffering he had been putting others through! But in spite of me having every reason to be afraid of this man, I went, knowing that Jesus would give me the strength I needed to serve him. When I got to the place where Saul was staying, I placed my hands on him, took a deep breath, and said, "Saul, the Lord Jesus has sent me. He is the same one who appeared to you along the road. He wants you to be able to see and to be filled with the Holy Spirit."

Suddenly something like fish scales fell from Saul's eyes, and he could see. I baptized him, and he had something to eat and felt much better.

Saul told me how his blindness came about. He was on his way to our city with permission to arrest any man or woman who had accepted the Lord's Way and take them to Jerusalem for trial. Just outside the city he suddenly saw a bright light from heaven, flashing around him. He fell on the ground and heard a voice say, "Saul! Saul! Why are you so cruel to me?"

Saul asked who it was, and the voice said, "I am Jesus. I am the one to whom you are so cruel. Now get up and go into the city, where you will be told what to do."

Saul had several men with him. They heard the voice but did not see anyone, and it left them speechless. When Saul got up from the ground, he could not see a thing, and his traveling companions had to lead him by the hand. He had been in the city for three days. His blindness so disturbed him that he did not eat or drink for those three days.

Now you may not recall who Saul was. You may have heard of him by the name of Paul. This was the name he became known by later. I'm glad Christ was able to use me to heal Saul, because he witnessed for Christ and then, after several years of reflection and study, he was able to be the main leader in spreading the gospel of Christ throughout the area around the Mediterranean Sea.

Christ worked miracles through one who had worked against the Christians. And Christ used me. Pretty miraculous that I was able to help! No matter who we are or what we have done, Christ can use us all.

All About Racing

1. When you run in a competition, you run a _____ .
2. The place that you begin a race is called the _____ line.
3. The place that you finish a race is called the _____ line.
4. When several people on a team take turns running, it is called a
   _____ .
5. The round or oval path that you take in a race is called the race _____ .
6. A short, fast race is called a _____ .
7. People who race together in groups are called _____ .
8. The winner of a foot race may receive a ribbon or a _____ .
9. When we are Christians, we simply run for _____ .

After he had been a missionary for Christ for many years, Paul
(whose original name was Saul) said, "I have finished the race,
and I have been faithful" (2 Timothy 4:7b). His race was not one
that was run; instead, it was a way of spreading the news of Christ.
He answered the call to work on the Christian team
after he met Christ on the road to Damascus. You can read
about that experience in Acts 9:1-19.

Reproducible 11C

BibleZone® LIVE

Choose one or more activities to immerse your children in the Bible story.

Reminder Crosses

Hand out **Reproducible 11D** and **click pen necklaces**. Read the information on the reproducible with the class.

Say: The cross has the names of some people who have answered Christ's call. When we try to live as God wants us to, we are answering Christ's call in some way. Put your name on the first line on your cross, and then we will all put our names on one another's crosses as reminders of how we must answer Christ's call.

After they have written their names on all the crosses, lay out masking tape, plastic wrap, watercolor or tempera paint, and trays or shallow dishes. Protect the tables and instruct the students to cover the cross with masking tape. They will crumple some plastic wrap in a ball and dab it in the paint and then dab it over the paper. Warn them not to wipe or brush with the plastic wrap, but to dab it. Encourage them to cover the page. They should leave the memory verse clear. When the paint is dry, they will remove the masking tape to reveal the cross underneath.

Supplies:
Reproducible 11D
masking tape
plastic wrap
watercolor or
    tempera paint
trays or shallow dishes
newspaper or other
    table protection
cleanup supplies

ZoneZillies®:
click pen necklaces

Are You the Disciple?

Divide the class into two teams—the Sauls and the Pauls. Distribute small pieces of paper and **click pen necklaces** and have each person quickly write down one thing that characterizes him or her as a disciple of Jesus. Instruct the students not to show anyone else what they have written. Collect the papers in a basket and encourage the students to listen carefully but not write anything down as you read through the papers twice.

The Sauls will go first. They will try to match a characteristic with a member of the other team, saying, "(*Name*), are you the disciple who (*read what is on the paper*)?" If they've made a correct match, that person joins their team, and the team continues until they fail to make a match. The Pauls then use the same words to call those who have become Sauls back again, and they attempt some other matches. Continue playing until everyone is on the same side.

Supplies:
small pieces of paper
basket

ZoneZillies®:
click pen necklaces

Life Zone

Choose one or more activities to bring the Bible to life.

Supplies:
page 174
Celebration Table
running shoes
Reproducible 11E
CD player

ZoneZillies®:
CD

Praise 'n Prayer

Play "The Servant Song" **(CD)** to call the class to the Celebration Table for Praise 'n Prayer.

Light the candle and call their attention to the appropriate seasonal color and the running shoes on the table.

Ask: Why do you suppose we have the running shoes on our Celebration Table? How do they remind you of our theme and Bible verse today?

Hand out **Reproducible 11E**, "Sing! Shout! Turn About!" **(CD)**. Encourage the students to sing it together.

Ask the student you assigned earlier to close with the following prayer (also on page 174): "Our God, help us to remember to follow what you call us to do. Sometimes we feel like it's hard to run the race, but we know that you will be with us all the way. Amen."

Make a copy of HomeZone® for each student in your class.

138

PENCIL HOLDER

Make a pencil holder that will also remind you to act as a disciple. You will need: an empty can with no sharp edges, a self-adhesive magnet strip, ribbon, and construction paper.

Cut construction paper (or you can use self-adhesive shelf liner) to fit around the can and cover it. Tape the paper around the can and tie the ribbon around the top of the can. Cut several one-inch circles from different colored paper and write some way that you can be a disciple on each circle.

Place a piece of self-adhesive magnet on each circle and stick it on the outside of a can. When you have done one of the disciple actions, move the circle to the inside of the can. When you think of something new to do, make a new circle.

ThinkZone

How can I be a disciple for Jesus? Why is it important for me to show others that I am a disciple of Jesus?

Memory Verse

[God] chose me to be a servant of Christ Jesus.
Romans 15:16, adapted

Veggie and Cheese Wrap

2 nine-inch flour tortillas
6 tablespoons cream cheese (room temperature)
½ cup mashed avocado (optional)
½ small peeled cucumber, sliced thinly
1 tomato, sliced thinly
1 cup alfalfa sprouts
salt and pepper

Spread tortillas with cream cheese and mashed avocado. Lay half of the cucumber slices on each tortilla. Place half the tomato slices on each tortilla over the cucumber slices. Sprinkle alfalfa sprouts over both tortillas. Working with one tortilla at a time, roll by folding about two inches of one edge over itself. Fold the same amount on the opposite edge. This gives you two straight sides and two rounded sides. Beginning with a rounded side, roll up tortilla. Hold the folded edges down as you roll it up completely. Place, seam side down, on a cutting board and cut in half on the diagonal. Makes 2 servings.

Jesus calls us to be disciples.

Christ's Team

Called to be members of the team:

Paul
Ananias
Peter
Luke

_____
_____
_____
_____
_____
_____
_____
_____
_____
_____
_____
_____

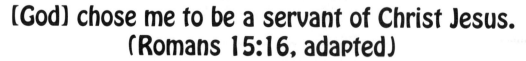

**(God) chose me to be a servant of Christ Jesus.
(Romans 15:16, adapted)**

Reproducible 11D

BibleZone® LIVE

Sing! Shout! Turn About!

Sing! (*Sing!*) Shout! (*Shout!*)
Turn about!
Let's turn to follow Jesus.
Let's Sing! (*Sing!*) Shout! (*Shout!*)
Turn about!
We'll follow where he leads us.

Traveling, traveling, Paul was sharing
God's Good News to all.
Turning, turning, mission burning
in Paul's heart to heed God's call.

Sing! (*Sing!*) Shout! (*Shout!*)
Turn about!
Let's turn to follow Jesus.
Let's Sing! (*Sing!*) Shout! (*Shout!*)
Turn about!
We'll follow where he leads us.

Turning, turning, we are learning
more of God each day.
Growing, growing, see us showing
how to follow Jesus' way.

Sing! (*Sing!*) Shout! (*Shout!*)
Turn about!
Let's turn to follow Jesus.
Let's Sing! (*Sing!*) Shout! (*Shout!*)
Turn about!
We'll follow where he leads us.

Changing, changing, rearranging,
always something new;
moving, moving and improving
as God calls us each to do.

Sing! (*Sing!*) Shout! (*Shout!*)
Turn about!
Let's turn to follow Jesus.
Let's Sing! (*Sing!*) Shout! (*Shout!*)
Turn about!
We'll follow where he leads us.

WORDS: St. 1 by Debi Tyree; sts. 2–3 by James Ritchie and Nylea L. Butler-Moore
MUSIC: Nylea L. Butler-Moore
Sts. 2–3 and music © 1993 Cokesbury; st. 1 © 1999 Cokesbury

Philip and the Ethiopian

Enter the

Bible Verse
Show me your paths and teach me to follow.

Psalm 25:4

Bible Story
Acts 8:26-40

Half of the first-century traffic in this part of the world passed along the road extending from Jerusalem, through Bethlehem and Hebron, and joining the main road to Egypt just south of Gaza. It was on this road that Philip met the man servant and chief treasurer of Candace, queen of Ethiopia. The road was not literally a desert route. But figuratively, since theological reflection and awareness of God's presence are often fostered in deserted places, it could qualify.

Teachers using the Contemporary English Version of the Bible avoid having to explain the word *eunuch* since the translators have elected not to use this description of the Ethiopian official, probably expecting that either the word itself or its definition would be a distraction to their intended audience. For your information, however, it remains important. This Ethiopian proselyte or convert to Judaism is like the transient who is fed on the front porch of the home, but not permitted inside. Because of his anatomical

incompleteness, the Ethiopian would never be welcomed into the Temple's Court of Israel. He would be restricted to the Court of the Gentiles open to anyone, regardless of their profession of faith. That was the Law.

We assume his proselyte status because of his sincere desire to understand the one God worshiped by the Hebrews in Jerusalem—a desire that had taken him a significant distance down the road from the temples dedicated to an assortment of gods in his own country. For him to be new to the faith and yet wrestling with the challenging prophecies of Isaiah—especially when even his understanding would not gain him full admission to the faith—is to his credit.

Using the Isaiah passage as a springboard to talk about Jesus and his message, Philip converted a chariot into a synagogue; and the Holy Spirit converted a man who would have always known exclusion under the Law into one fully included in the community of faith by the grace of Jesus Christ.

Disciples of Jesus share the good news with others.

Scope the

ZONE	TIME	SUPPLIES	◎ ZONEZILLIES®
Zoom Into the Zone			
Get in the Zone	5 minutes	CD player	CD
Celebration Table	5 minutes	page 174, small table, white tablecloth, colored fabric, candle, Bible, ruler	none
Puzzled Bible Verse	5 minutes	Reproducible 12C, pencils, Bibles	none
BibleZone®			
Turn to the Bible	5 minutes	Bibles, bookmarks	spiked rubber ball
Enjoy the Story	10 minutes	Reproducibles 12A–12B	spiked rubber ball
Good News Collage	10 minutes	posterboard, magazines, paper, scissors, markers, glue	none
Streets and Alleys	5 minutes	none	train whistle
LifeZone			
Find the Path	5 minutes	Reproducible 12D, markers	none
Praise 'n Prayer	10 minutes	Celebration Table, page 174, ruler, Reproducible 12E, CD player	spiked rubber ball, CD

◎ ZoneZillies® are found in the **BibleZone® LIVE FUNspirational® Kit.**

Zoom Into the Zone

Choose one or more activities to catch your children's interest.

Supplies:
CD player

ZoneZillies®:
CD

Get in the Zone

Play "Hallelujah Chorus" **(CD)** as the students arrive. Greet each student with a happy smile.

Say: Welcome to BibleZone Live! I'm glad you are here. This is the fun place where we will get to know the Bible as our book!

Supplies:
page 174
small table
white tablecloth
colored fabric
candle
Bible
ruler

ZoneZillies®:
none

Celebration Table

Ask one of the students who arrives early to help you prepare the Celebration Table.

Cover the table and add a candle, a Bible, and colored fabric appropriate to the season, according to the instructions on page 12.

For this session place a ruler beside the candle.

Ask a student to prepare to read the closing prayer during your Praise 'n Prayer time. Give that student a copy of the prayer for week twelve (page 174).

Supplies:
Reproducible 12C
pencils
Bibles

ZoneZillies®:
none

Puzzled Bible Verse

Hand out Bibles, **Reproducible 12C**, and pencils. Be sure that the students understand the directions. The students will write the numbers 1–9 consecutively into each vertical column. There are some numbers already in each column to guide the students.

Once the children have placed the numbers in the puzzle, they will find the Bible verse by filling in the corresponding words in the row marked with an asterisk.

Choose one or more activities to immerse your children in the Bible story.

Turn to the Bible

Hand out Bibles and bookmarks. Ask the students to find Isaiah 53:7–8 and put a bookmark in it. Then ask them to find Acts 8:32–33.

Ask someone to read each passage aloud as the others follow along silently. Use the **spiked rubber ball** to guide discussion as to how these passages are alike and how they are different.

If they question the differences, point out that Luke, the author of Acts, probably didn't have a copy of Isaiah in front of him as he wrote, but was working from memory as he recalled how the story of Philip and the Ethiopian official had been told to him.

Supplies:
Bibles
bookmarks

ZoneZillies®:
spiked rubber ball

Enjoy the Story

Hand out **Reproducibles 12A–12B** and read the story together. After reading the story use the **spiked rubber ball** to initiate discussion.

Ask: Have you ever felt that you should do something, but you didn't know why? Did you do it? How did it turn out?

Supplies:
Reproducibles
12A–12B

ZoneZillies®:
spiked rubber ball

God Leads

(*based on Acts 8:26-40*)

by Delia Halverson

Have you ever had the feeling that you should do something, but you didn't know why? That's just what happened to me.

My name is Philip, and I was a disciple of Jesus from the beginning. Though I wasn't one of the twelve, I was still very close—close enough to miss him terribly when he died. Of course I was happy—although a bit confused—to learn that he had risen from the dead, and it was great to have him with us again for a while after his resurrection.

Before leaving us and ascending into heaven, Jesus challenged us to spread his message to everyone. No big deal, you say? What about the enemies of Jesus who continued to search out his followers? Admitting to being a follower of Jesus took guts, so that really was a challenge!

One day I felt the presence of God and an angel of the Lord telling me, "Go south along the desert road that leads from Jerusalem to Gaza." This wasn't actually a road going through the desert, but I'm not one to argue with angels.

People have experienced God in amazing ways in desert places, so maybe it was a "desert thing" that God had planned for the road. So I had lots of unanswered questions, but I also had the feeling that I should do it, even though I didn't know just why.

As it turns out, a court official of the queen of Ethiopia was traveling in a chariot along the road where I was walking. He had been in Jerusalem worshiping God, and this interested me since he was most likely raised with a belief in many gods. But he had embraced faith in the one true God, and he was eager to learn more about whom God was and what God was like.

I'm not sure that I would start reading the prophet Isaiah if I were new to the faith, but that's exactly what the Ethiopian was doing when I met up with him on his way back home—reading Isaiah out loud. God's Spirit gave me a nudge to talk with him. So I caught up with his chariot and called out to him, "Do you understand what you are reading?"

The Ethiopian answered me, "How can I understand unless someone helps me?" He invited me to get into his chariot and sit beside him as he read, "'He was led like a sheep on its way to be killed. He was silent as a lamb whose wool is being cut off, and he did not say a word. He was treated like a nobody and did not receive a fair trial. How can he have children, if his life is snatched away?'"

He asked me whether the prophet was talking about himself or about someone else, and I knew that I had a perfect opportunity to talk with him about Jesus.

So I started in with that passage and

Reproducible 12A

Permission granted to photocopy for local church use. © 2005 Abingdon Press.

explained to him my belief that the Messiah the prophet was talking about was a man I had known personally, a man named Jesus. I told him all about Jesus and what he had taught me.

I told him about the changes Jesus had made in my life; and I explained how knowing Jesus made a difference in the type of person I was, in how I treated others, and how I understood God and God's love. Before knowing Jesus, I had felt pretty much like a nobody, but he helped me feel like a very important somebody.

I told the Ethiopian that there were many of us who believed in Jesus who were coming together regularly to worship God. I told him that when someone became a member of our group, he or she was baptized with water. Without water, there could be no life as we know it.

The waters of baptism brought us a new life—a life filled with hope rather than the despair we had been living with under Roman rule and under our religious leaders. That baptism represented a promise to follow the way that Jesus taught—the way that leads us to a God of love.

About that time we rode by some water, and the Ethiopian called out, "Look! Here is some water. Why can't I be baptized?" He commanded that the chariot be stopped. We went into the water, and I baptized him, right then and there.

The Ethiopian went on his way, rejoicing, all ready to spread the good news with others in his country. That was the last we saw of each other, but I immediately had other opportunities much like this one. From Azotus to Caesarea, I went from town to town, telling people about Jesus.

Feelings, voices—sometimes you've just got to listen to them and trust that God has something important for us to do. I didn't know why I should go on that road to Gaza, but I knew that God had a reason. The good news of Jesus needed to be shared, and God was allowing me to be a part of the sharing.

Reproducible 12B

147

A Numbers Puzzle

Solve this numbers puzzle and discover our Bible verse for today.
Fill in the squares by listing the numbers 1 through 9 consecutively down the page.
For example, the first column will be 2 3 4 5 6 7 8 9 1. Each row and each column
will have one each of the numbers 1 through 9, but no number should be repeated.
Then use the number key below to fill in the words on the row marked
with an asterisk. Look up Psalm 25:4 to check your answer.

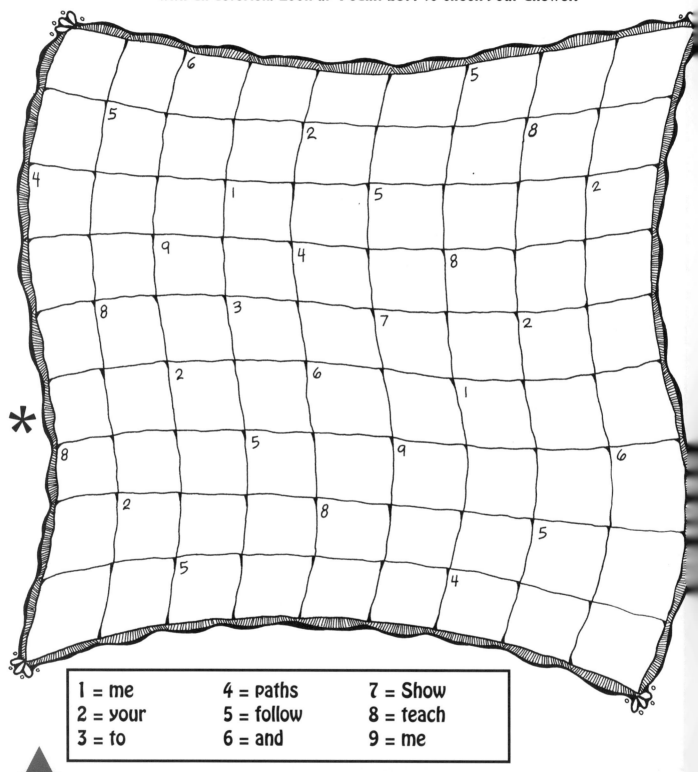

1 = me	4 = paths	7 = Show
2 = your	5 = follow	8 = teach
3 = to	6 = and	9 = me

Reproducible 12C

BibleZone® LIVE

Choose one or more activities to immerse your children in the Bible story.

Good News Collage

At the top of a sheet of posterboard, write "Sharing the Good News." Hand out magazines, blank paper, scissors, markers, and glue. Ask the students to look through the magazines or draw pictures that show ways we can share the good news of Jesus. Help them see that the good news can be shared while they are working or in school, when they play sports, or in other occasions. Include pictures of people helping sick persons, older children playing with younger children, and other occasions. Have the students glue the pictures randomly across the posterboard, filling up the space except where the lettering is. Display the poster in the church building.

Supplies:
posterboard
magazines
paper
scissors
markers
glue

ZoneZillies®:
none

Streets and Alleys

For this game it is best to have twelve players or more, and you will need plenty of space. Select a runner and a chaser. If you have more than twelve players, also select a caller. If not, you may serve as the caller. Ask the remaining players to line up in three rows all facing in the same direction, and have them hold hands while keeping the rows about five feet apart. The spaces between the rows are called "streets."

The chaser will chase the runner through these "streets." The runner starts at the end of the street farthest to the left. The chaser, who is several feet away, chases the runner through the course. The caller will give the signal to begin using the **train whistle**.

At any time, the caller may shout, "Alleys!" On this signal the rows immediately drop hands, turn to the right, and join hands with their new neighbors, thereby creating new rows with the space between the new rows as the "alleys." The runner and chaser will quickly change directions and continue the chase. When the caller calls "Streets!" the players again turn to the right, forming the streets. The runner and chaser must not duck under arms or run outside the playing area. The caller will randomly call "Streets!" or "Alleys!" and the runner and chaser continue. When the runner is caught, the runner, chaser, and caller take places in the line; and other players become the runner, chaser, and caller. Each new game begins in the "streets" formation. After playing the game, talk about it with the class.

Ask: How did this game make you think about choices? What would have happened if you had made the wrong choices? How does the game remind you of our Bible verse?

Supplies:
none

ZoneZillies®:
train whistle

Supplies:
Reproducible 12D
markers

ZoneZillies®:
none

Find the Path

Hand out **Reproducible 12D** and markers. Be sure that the students understand the directions. When the reproducible is completed, there will be one color that stands out as a continuous path through the maze.

After they have finished, ask if one path stands out from the rest and whether the maze reminds them of the Bible verse for today.

Supplies:
Celebration Table
page 174
ruler
Reproducible 12E
CD player

ZoneZillies®:
spiked rubber ball
CD

Praise 'n Prayer

Play "The Servant Song" **(CD)** to call the class to the Celebration Table for Praise 'n Prayer. Light the candle and call their attention to the appropriate seasonal color and the ruler on the table. Ask them to say the Bible verse together. Use the **spiked rubber ball** to guide conversation.

Ask: How is a ruler a symbol of this Bible verse? (*A ruler is a guide that we use to draw a straight line, and the Bible verse tells us to ask God to guide us in the way God wants us to go.*)

Hand out **Reproducible 12E**, "It Makes No Difference" **(CD),** and read the words together first. Point out that instead of saying "It makes no difference . . .," the last verse clearly states "It makes a difference." Play the verse through once to familiarize yourselves with the tune. Then sing the song together.

Ask the student you assigned earlier to close with the following prayer (also on page 174): "Our God, we want to follow your paths, but sometimes we forget. Help us to remember to ask just what you want us to do. Amen."

Make a copy of HomeZone® for each student in your class.

COOKIE BOX

Make a cookie box from two matching disposable plastic containers to use as a gift box for the cookies below.

Either find pictures or draw pictures on paper to fit the three sides of one disposable plastic container. Cut three pictures to fit the sides of one of the containers so that the edges slightly overlap the corners. Cut plain paper to fit the fourth side and print a Bible verse on the paper. A possible Bible verse is: "Christ gives me the strength to face anything" (Philippians 4:13).

Lightly place one container inside the other and slide the pictures and Bible verse paper down between the two containers to cover the four sides. When the pictures and Bible verse are in the right place, press the inner container down to keep the pictures in place. Fill the inner container with cookies and press the lid on the top. A sticky bow in the center of the lid will make a nice gift that shares the good news of Jesus with others.

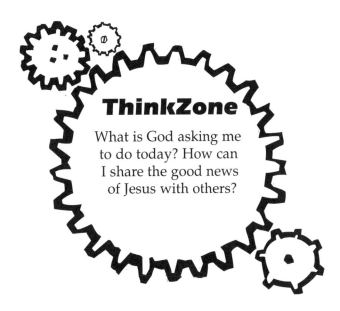

ThinkZone

What is God asking me to do today? How can I share the good news of Jesus with others?

Memory Verse

Show me your paths and teach me to follow.
Psalm 25:4

Cookies to Share

Mix the following and set it aside:
3 cups flour
1 teaspoon baking powder
½ teaspoon salt

Cream together:
1 cup butter
½ cup sugar

Add to the creamed mixture and beat:
1 egg
2 tablespoons milk
1 teaspoon vanilla

Add the flour mixture and mix well. Refrigerate overnight. Roll the dough out and cut into shapes.

Bake at 400 degrees for 4–5 minutes. Makes about three dozen average-size cookies.

Disciples of Jesus share the good news with others.

Follow God's Path

Color the sections on the design according to the key below.
When you have finished, you will find that one path leads to
the finish. Which color is the right path?

Y=Yellow B=Blue R = Red G = Green P=Purple

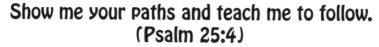

Show me your paths and teach me to follow.
(Psalm 25:4)

Reproducible 12D

BIBLEZONE® LIVE

Song Zone

It Makes No Difference

It makes no difference who we are,
what language we may speak;
God loves us all and hears our prayers—
he knows our needs and cares.

It makes no difference where we live,
in city, town, or farm;
God loves us all and hears our prayers—
he knows our needs and cares.

It makes no difference how we look,
what color is our skin;
God loves us all and hears our prayers—
he knows our needs and cares.

It makes a difference how we treat
our neighbors and our friends;
God loves us all and hears our prayers—
he knows our needs and cares.

WORDS: Doris Clare Demaree; adapted by Bert Polman, 1993
MUSIC: Sean E. Ivory, 1993
Words © 1994, CRC Publications
Music © 1994 Sean E. Ivory

Barnabas

Enter the ZONE

Bible Verse

Encourage anyone who feels left out, help all who are weak, and be patient with everyone.

1 Thessalonians 5:14

Bible Story

Acts 4:32-37; 9:26-31; 11:19-30

If there had not been Barnabas, a lesser recognized follower of Jesus, we might not know Paul in the way that we do. When he is first mentioned in the Scripture, Barnabas proves his dedication to the Lord and to Christ's message by selling his field and bringing the money to the apostles to go into the common fund for the Christians.

Living up to the name "Barnabas" or "encourager" given to him by early church leaders, this early Christian was among the followers in Jerusalem when Paul first made his appearance before them. When these leaders rejected Paul, Barnabas took Paul under his wing and vouched for him—risking his reputation for one who had previously been a feared enemy.

Though Paul is credited with strengthening the church at Antioch, a close reading of Acts 11:19-30 shows Barnabas as the encourager behind the scenes. After Stephen's death, Christians scattered so that they were not as easy to find, but they continued to speak Christ's message. Not convinced that Christ's message was for the Gentiles, their primary audience was Jews. Remember that the Gospels, which pulled all of his teachings together and spoke of the times when Jesus took the word to Gentiles, were not yet written.

When Jerusalem church leaders heard about men from Cyprus and Cyrene courageously spreading the word among Gentiles in Antioch, they sent Barnabas to see what was going on. The "encourager" was able to smooth out the rough edges and then bring Paul in to help. Their combined guidance made for a strong church in Antioch, where believers were first known as Christians.

Luke tells of a later mission trip (Acts 15) where Paul and Barnabas disagreed and parted company. Barnabas then took John Mark under his wing to encourage him. Like Barnabas, we teachers often find ourselves offering behind-the-scenes encouragement, contributing quietly to the spreading of good news.

Disciples of Jesus encourage one another.

Scope the

ZONE	TIME	SUPPLIES	⊚ ZONEZILLIES®
Zoom Into the Zone			
Get in the Zone	5 minutes	CD player	CD
Celebration Table	5 minutes	page 174, small table, white tablecloth, colored fabric, candle, Bible, mirror	none
Find the Verse	10 minutes	Bibles, paper with a glossy surface	click pen necklaces
BibleZone®			
Enjoy the Story	10 minutes	Reproducibles 13A–13B	none
Barnabas Game	10 minutes	Reproducibles 13C and 13D, pages 168 and 169, tape, game pieces, scissors	none
Straw Painting	10 minutes	tempera paint, plastic cups, eye droppers or spoons, plastic drinking straws, Bible verse papers	none
Human Spelling Bee	5 minutes	CD player, Reproducible 13E, chalkboard and chalk or large piece of paper and marker	CD
LifeZone			
Praise 'n Prayer	10 minutes	Celebration Table, page 174, mirror, Reproducible 13E, CD player	spiked rubber ball, CD

⊚ ZoneZillies® are found in the **BibleZone® LIVE FUNspirational® Kit.**

Zoom Into the Zone

Choose one or more activities to catch your children's interest.

Supplies:
CD player

ZoneZillies®:
CD

Get in the Zone

Play "Hallelujah Chorus" **(CD)** as the students arrive. Greet each student with a happy smile.

Say: Welcome to BibleZone Live! I'm glad you are here. This is the fun place where we will get to know the Bible as our book!

Supplies:
page 174
small table
white tablecloth
colored fabric
candle
Bible
mirror

ZoneZillies®:
none

Celebration Table

Ask one of the students who arrives early to help you prepare the Celebration Table.

Cover the table and add a candle, a Bible, and colored fabric appropriate to the season, according to the instructions on page 12.

For this session place a mirror beside the candle.

Ask a student to prepare to read the closing prayer during your Praise 'n Prayer time. Give that student a copy of the prayer for week thirteen (page 174).

Supplies:
Bibles
paper with a glossy
    surface

ZoneZillies®:
click pen necklaces

Find the Verse

Hand out Bibles and ask the students to work in pairs to find 1 Thessalonians 5:14. Read the verse together several times. Hand out the **click pen necklaces** and 8½-by-11 sheets of paper with a glossy surface. Have each student write the verse in large letters on the paper. Have them write their names on the back and then put them aside for later.

156

Choose one or more activities to immerse your children in the Bible story.

Enjoy the Story

Hand out **Reproducibles 13A–13B**. Note that the story is told by using each letter of "Barnabas, Son of Encouragement" as the beginning of a sentence.

This method, called acrostic writing, was used for some of the Psalms in the Hebrew language.

Supplies:
Reproducibles
13A–13B

ZoneZillies®:
none

Barnabas Game

Divide the class into groups of three to five persons. Hand out **Reproducibles 13C** and **13D**, photocopies of the number cube on page 168, photocopies of the game cards on page 169, and game pieces (coins, tokens, construction paper squares, and so forth).

Give each group time to tape the two halves of their game boards together.

The number cube will be used to determine the number of spaces to move. Have each group mix up their set of game cards. These will be drawn whenever someone lands on a X.

The player who lands on that space will follow the directions on the card. Ask the students to place the cards face down on a table, each set in its own pile. Have them play the game.

Supplies:
Reproducibles 13C
    and 13D
pages 168 and 169
tape
game pieces
scissors

ZoneZillies®:

Barnabas Was His Name

(based on Acts 4:32-37; 9:26-31; 11:19-30)

by Delia Halverson

B Believers of Jesus were of one heart and soul, and no one claimed private ownership of any possessions.

A All of the followers brought their things together, and they held everything in common. No one was in need because they all shared.

R Recognizing the importance of Jesus, a man named Joseph, a Levite who was a native of Cyprus, sold his field and brought the money to the apostles.

N Names tell much about a person, and they called this man Barnabas, which means "Son of Encouragement." He encouraged others in every way.

A A man named Saul, formerly a persecutor of the believers, became a follower of Jesus. When he came to Jerusalem to join the disciples, they did not believe him.

B Barnabas encouraged the apostles to accept Paul, describing how Saul had seen the Lord, had heard the Lord speak to him, and had spoken boldly in the name of Jesus.

A After Barnabas' encouragement, Saul (who was also called Paul) went in and out among the disciples in Jerusalem, speaking boldly in the name of the Lord.

S Saul spoke and argued with the religious authorities, and they attempted to kill him.

S Some of the believers took Saul to Caesarea and sent him off to Tarsus, so that he would not be killed.

O Others in the churches throughout Judea, Galilee, and Samaria had peace and increased in number.

N Now there had been a disciple named Stephen who was martyred or killed for his faith, which caused many followers of Jesus to flee to other countries—some as far as Phoenicia, Cyprus, and Antioch. They spread the word among the Jews there.

Reproducible 13A

BibleZone® LIVI

O On coming to Antioch, some began telling those who were not Jews about the Lord Jesus, and a great number became followers of Jesus.

F From Antioch, the news of these followers of Jesus, who were not Jews, came to Jerusalem. The leaders of the church in Jerusalem sent Barnabas to Antioch.

E Even though these believers in Antioch were not Jews, Barnabas saw that they were filled with the grace of God.

N Now Barnabas rejoiced and told them to remain faithful to God. Barnabas was an encourager. Many people became believers.

C Continuing to grow, the fellowship in Antioch became larger. Barnabas went to Tarsus to find Saul and brought him back to Antioch.

O Over the next year Barnabas and Saul met with the church and taught a great many people.

U Until then, the followers of Jesus were called The Way, but in Antioch they were called Christians for the first time.

R Ready for action, the Christian community grew in Antioch.

A At that time prophets came down from Jerusalem to Antioch.

G Gaining opportunity, a prophet named Agabus stood up and predicted a famine.

E Even all parts of the world were to have this famine.

M Meeting together, the disciples decided that they would send relief to the believers in Judea.

E Each person gave according to his or her ability.

N Now they needed someone to take what they had given to Judea.

T They selected Barnabas and Saul to take their gifts to the elders of the church in Judea.

159

START

Reproducible 13C

BIBLEZONE® LIV

Choose one or more activities to immerse your children in the Bible story.

Straw Painting

Lay out plastic cups of tempera paint, eye droppers or plastic spoons, and plastic drinking straws. Explain that you will decorate the Bible verse page that they wrote earlier by dripping several colors of tempera paint on the paper with an eye dropper or spoon; and using a straw, blow the paint in different directions until it is spread across the page.

NOTE: Watch for dizziness and encourage the students to rest between blows.

Supplies:
tempera paint
plastic cups
eye droppers or
    spoons
plastic drinking straws
Bible verse papers

ZoneZillies®:
none

Human Spelling Bee

Hand out **Reproducible 13E**, "I Am a 'C'" **(CD)**. Listen to the song and sing it together several times.

Say: As Christians we encourage others, just as Barnabas encouraged those who were becoming Christian. We are going to experiment with ways to shape our bodies to form the letters of the word *Christian.*

Write the word in capital letters on a chalkboard or a large piece of paper and have everyone stand. Take the letters one at a time and experiment with forming the letters with your bodies. Then ask for volunteers for each letter. Have them stand in a line according to their letters. If your class is small, you can assign two letters for a student.

Play and sing the song again, but during the singing each person with that letter will form the letter when it is sung.

Supplies:
CD player
Reproducible 13E
chalkboard and chalk
    or large piece of
    paper and marker

ZoneZillies®:
CD

Life Zone

Choose one or more activities to bring the Bible to life.

Supplies:
Celebration Table
page 174
mirror
Reproducible 13E
CD player

ZoneZillies®:
spiked rubber ball
CD

Praise 'n Prayer

Play "The Servant Song" **(CD)** to call the class to the Celebration Table for Praise 'n Prayer.

Light the candle and call their attention to the appropriate seasonal color and mirror on the table.

Use the **spiked rubber ball** to ask the students why we have the mirror on the Celebration Table.

Remind the students that when they look into a mirror, they should ask themselves if they are encouragers—if they encourage others or put them down.

Sing "I Am a C" **(CD; Reproducible 13E)** again.

Ask the student you assigned earlier to close with the following prayer (also on page 174): "Our God, help us to remember to encourage others. When others are put down, remind us that such actions hurt, and give us words of encouragement. Amen."

Make a copy of HomeZone® for each student in your class.

CHRISTIAN SHRINKER

Ask an adult to help you with this project. Preheat your oven to 275 degrees.

With a permanent marker, draw the outline of a design on a large plastic lid. Cut out the design and outline the edge with a permanent marker. Using the marker, draw a large C in the center of the design. Using different permanent markers, decorate the design in any other way you'd like. Use a paper punch to punch two holes in the top of the design, overlapping to make one large hole. You may make several of these designs to share with others. Cover a cookie sheet with aluminum foil and place the designs on the foil. Put the cookie sheet of designs in the oven. If the designs begin to curl, press them flat with a spatula or stick, or reduce the temperature of the oven a little. When the plastic has shrunken and is flat, remove the cookie sheet from the oven. Press the design with a spatula. Thread yarn through the hole to hang the shrinker.

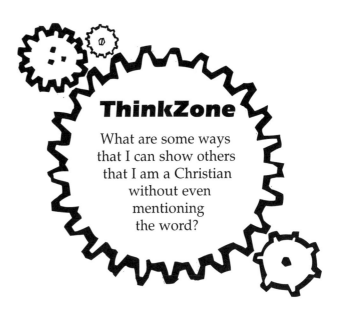

ThinkZone

What are some ways that I can show others that I am a Christian without even mentioning the word?

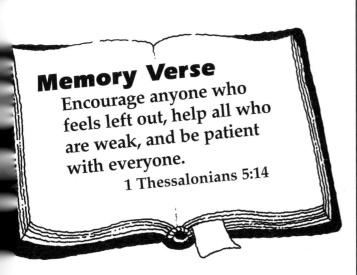

Memory Verse

Encourage anyone who feels left out, help all who are weak, and be patient with everyone.

1 Thessalonians 5:14

Shaped Cheese Macs

You will need 1 pound pasta; 4 quarts (16 cups) water; 1 teaspoon salt; 3 tablespoons butter; 3 tablespoons flour; 1½ cups milk; 1½ cups shredded sharp cheddar cheese; and 2 tablespoons grated Parmesan cheese (optional).

Melt butter over medium heat, stirring. Add flour and whisk until bubbly but not brown. Keeping the pan on the heat and stirring with the whisk, slowly add milk. Cook, whisking until mixture is smooth, thick, and gently boiling. Remove from heat and add cheddar and Parmesan cheeses. Whisk until the cheeses melt. Cover the pan and set it aside. Place water and salt in a pot and place on the stove on high. Bring the water to a boil. Slowly add pasta and stir. Boil, uncovered, until tender. Stir occasionally. Drain. Add the pasta to the sauce and stir until blended. Serve immediately or place in a greased dish in a warm oven until ready to serve.

Disciples of Jesus encourage one another.

FINISH

Reproducible 13D

BIBLEZONE® LIVE

I Am a "C"

I am a C, I am a C-H,
I am a C-H-R-I-S-T-I-A-N;
and I have C-H-R-I-S-T in my H-E-A-R-T
and I will L-I-V-E E-T-E-R-N-A-L-L-Y.

WORDS: Traditional
MUSIC: Traditional; arr. Lyndell Leatherman
Arr. © 1980 Lillenas Publishing Company (SESAC).
All rights reserved.
Administered by The Copyright Company, 40 Music Square East, Nashville, TN 37203

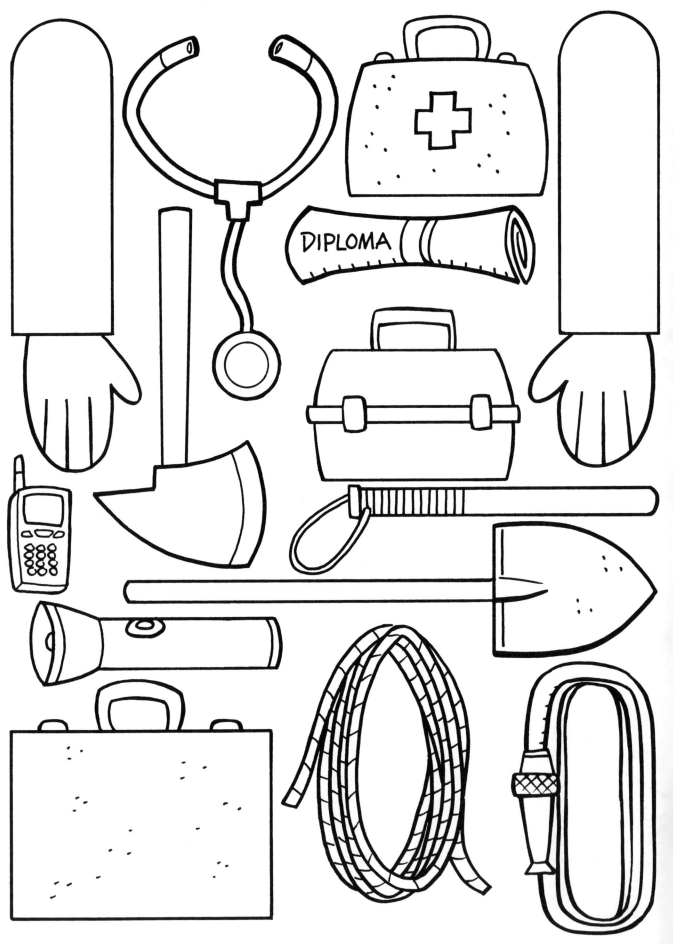

DIPLOMA

BIBLEZONE® LIVE

Cut out the number cube
along the solid lines. Fold
along the dotted lines.
Glue or tape together to
form a cube. Use the
cube with the gameboard.

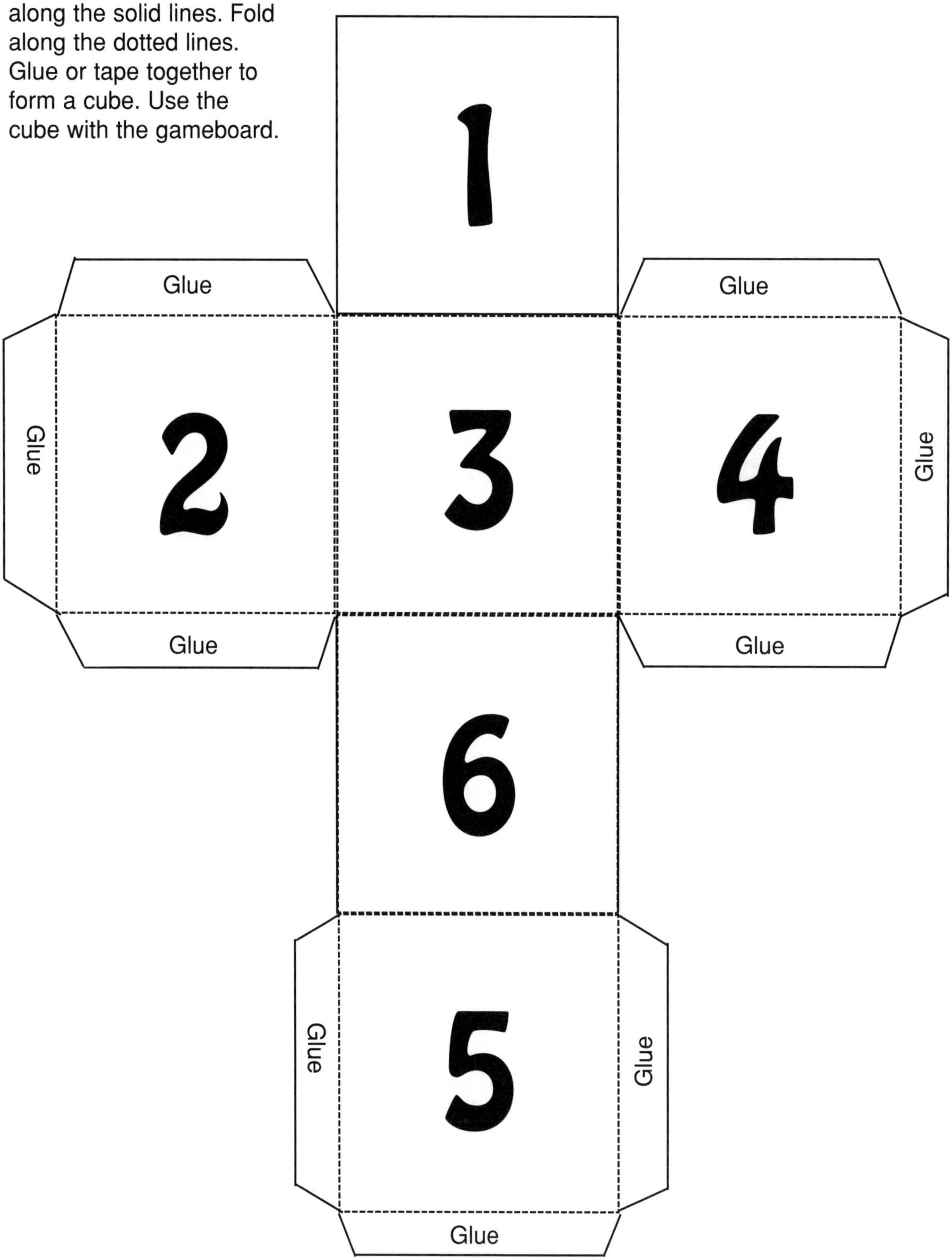

1

Glue

Glue

Glue

Glue

2

3

4

Glue

Glue

Glue

6

Glue

Glue

5

Glue

BIBLEZONE® LIVI

Your little sister is learning
to climb the stairs, and you hold
her hand. Go ahead 1 space.

You helped a classmate
understand a math problem.
Go ahead 1 space.

You made fun of someone
who missed a spelling word.
Go back 2 spaces.

You crossed the street
in order not to meet someone
who has a learning disability.
Go back 4 spaces.

You asked someone who is not
a very good soccer player
to play on your team, and you
cheered when he kicked
the ball. Go ahead 2 spaces.

You took time to go to a nursing
home and talk to someone who is
lonely. Go ahead 1 space.

You put someone down,
making fun of the
way she talked. Go back 1 space.

You wrote a note to your teacher,
saying how much you enjoyed
class. Go ahead 3 spaces.

BibleZone **LIVE**

_____

BibleZone **LIVE**

_____

BibleZone **LIVE**

_____

BibleZone **LIVE**

_____

BibleZone **LIVE**

_____

BibleZone **LIVE**

_____

BibleZone **LIVE**

_____

BibleZone **LIVE**

_____

BibleZone® LIVE

The Load for the Road

Write the following verse on the chalkboard, on a markerboard, or on a sheet of newsprint. Underline the fourth line or write it in a different color than the first three.

We're headed down the road,
And we've packed up quite a load.
On the trek that we are making,
See the _____ I am (*name* is) taking.

Give each person a slip of paper and a **click pen necklace**. Ask each student to write an item on the slip of paper that he or she might take on a road trip. This might include a map, a bottle of water, a change of clothing, and so forth. Tell each student to remember what he or she wrote. Have the students place the pens around their necks and place the paper slips in a backpack. Make sure that you have placed a slip of paper in the backpack as well.

Start a rhythm for the verse by having the students tap their feet—left, right, left, right . . .

Say: We will do the first three lines together, and then I will do the fourth line by myself and say what I am taking on our road trip. I'll toss the backpack to someone else, and we'll say the verse again. The person who catches the backpack will do the last line. You are going to need to remember what everyone is taking, and you'll only hear it once.

We are headed down the road, and we've packed up quite a load.
Left   right   left   right   left   right   left   right

On the trek that we are making, see the _____ I am taking.
Left   right   left   right   left   right left   right

Continue until all the students have said what they are taking on the road trip. Start again. While the students are saying the first three lines, take a slip of paper from the backpack. You will have to remember who said they were taking each item. When it comes to the fourth line, you will say, "See the lunch that Todd is taking." If Todd is the one taking the lunch, pass him the backpack and have him select a slip of paper. If Todd is not the one taking the lunch, the verse will be said again, and you will have to make another guess at who is taking the lunch. Continue until all the slips have been read and correctly connected with the persons who wrote them.

Make "I Believe" Bracelets

Ahead of time, cut off the sloping neck of several 16-ounce plastic soda bottles. Be sure that the bottles have removable labels so that the plastic has no printing. Students may do the additional cuts in class if they have strong, sharp scissors.

Say: Cut straight down the side on the bottle to the bottom. Then cut two identical rings per person from the bottles, cutting half-inch wide strips around the bottle, starting at the cut side. Cut a piece of construction paper the size of the bracelet and use a permanent pen to write "I am a follower of Jesus" on the paper. Glue any trim you would like to the edges of the paper. Place the paper between the two plastic strips from the soda bottle and punch a hole at each end through the three layers. Put a piece of yarn through the holes to tie the ends together. The yarn can be adjusted to the proper size to allow you to slip it on over your hand.

Thankful Collage

Make a collage of different things for which the students want to thank God. At the top of a large piece of paper, print "God, I Thank You." Have the students cut pictures from magazines that show things they are thankful for and glue them on the page, overlapping the pictures so that the page is solid with pictures.

Put the collage in a place where the church members can see it.

Take one giant step toward Emmaus, then pause.	Time flies as you're talking. Move three steps ahead.
Your sandals are slipping, take one little step.	Turn back toward Jerusalem. Go forward one step.
Step right and then left as you chat with a friend.	Take two small steps and stumble on rocks. Take one step back.
A stranger has joined you. Move two steps ahead.	A snake in your path! Sidestep twice, then take one step back.
Your grief slows your progress. Go back two large steps.	Emmaus ahead! Big step, little step, big step.

Week 1
O God, make us willing to serve rather than asking to be served, and help us find the joy of putting Jesus first, others second, and ourselves last. Amen.

Week 2
Our God, we praise you, and we thank you for sending Jesus, the Messiah. Amen.

Week 3
Our God, we want to be servants for you. Help us to know how to help others. Amen.

Week 4
Our God, we want to learn more about you and to know your presence every moment of our lives. Help us to be like Jesus, growing in faith and standing up for what we believe. Amen.

Week 5
Our God, forgive us for those times when we understand you as being anything less than awesome. Help us to see your awesomeness in everything around us. Fill us with awe as we consider how you raised Jesus from death. Amen.

Week 6
Our God, we thank you that we are followers of Jesus and that we know that Jesus is alive. Amen.

Week 7
Our God, we thank you for those whom Jesus sent out to tell others about you. Help us to share what we have learned with others. Amen.

Week 8
Our God, you are so great. Help us to be like the leper who remembered to return and thank Jesus for the healing. We want to always remember all that you do for us and your love for us. Amen.

Week 9
Our God, some think that being different means being better than others, and some think it means being worse. Help us to remember that you think we are all special, and remind us that we are called and prepared to do special things for you. Amen.

Week 10
Our God, we thank you that we can ask you for help. We know that you will help us even in hard times and that sometimes you send others to help us. Amen.

Week 11
Our God, help us to remember to follow what you call us to do. Sometimes we feel like it's hard to run the race, but we know that you will be with us all the way. Amen.

Week 12
Our God, we want to follow your paths, but sometimes we forget. Help us to remember to ask just what you want us to do. Amen.

Week 13
Our God, help us to remember to encourage others. When others are put down, remind us that such actions hurt, and give us words of encouragement. Amen.

BibleZone® Livi

LIVE

Use the following scale to rate BibleZone® LIVE resources
If you did not use a section, write "Did not use" in the Comments space.

1 = In No Lessons   2 = In Some Lessons   3 = In Most Lessons   4 = In All Lessons

1. *Enter the Zone* provided information that helped me
   teach this lesson's Scripture.

   1   2   3   4   Comments:

2. The *Scope the Zone* chart made lesson planning easy.

   1   2   3   4   Comments:

3. The teaching plan was organized in a way that made it
   easy to use.

   1   2   3   4   Comments:

4. The Teacher's Guide provided easy-to-follow instructions
   for the learning activities.

   1   2   3   4   Comments:

5. The supplies necessary to do the activities were easily
   located in my home or church.

   1   2   3   4   Comments:

6. My students were able to understand the lesson's
   ZoneIn®.

   1   2   3   4   Comments:

7. The activities matched the learning level and abilities
   of my students.

   1   2   3   4   Comments:

8. The number of activities in the lesson plan worked for the
   time I had available (indicate how much time):_____.
   If not, check:_____ too many _____too few.

   1   2   3   4   Comments:

9. I used activities from the GameZone® section of the
   Teacher's Guide.

   1   2   3   4   Comments:

10. I used activities from the ArtZone® section of the
    Teacher's Guide.

    1   2   3   4   Comments:

11. I used the CD in my classroom.

    1   2   3   4   Comments:

12. I used items from the BibleZone® LIVE
    FUNspirational® Kit.

    1   2   3   4   Comments:

13. I sent the HomeZone® page home to parents.

    1   2   3   4   Comments:

14. Other stories I would like to see in
    BibleZone® LIVE are:

ADDITIONAL COMMENTS

UNIT TITLE: ON THE ROAD

Activities my students enjoy the most are:

Activities my students enjoy the least are:

I use BibleZone® Live for_____Sunday School _____Second Hour Sunday School _____Children's Church

_____Wednesday nights _____Sunday nights _____Children's Fellowship _____other

ABOUT MY CLASS

Number of children at each age in my class:

_____Grade 4 _____Grade 5 _____Grade 6

_____Other (Specify)_____

Average number of children who attend my class each week:_____

I teach: _____alone _____with another teacher each week

_____taking turns with other teachers _____with an adult helper

ABOUT MY CHURCH

_____Rural _____Small Town _____Downtown _____Suburban

_____Under 200 Members _____200-700 Members _____Over 700 Members

Church Name and Address: _____

_____

My Name and Address: _____

_____

Please return this form to **Children's Marketing Business Unit**
201 8th Ave., So.
P.O. Box 801
Nashville, TN 37202-0801